Activating a Teaching–Learning Philosophy

A Practical Guide for Educators

ERLENE GRISE-OWENS, J. JAY MILLER, LARRY W. OWENS

Alexandria, Virginia

ISBN 978-0-87293-182-4

Printed in the United States of America on acid-free paper that meets the American National Standards Institute Z39-48 standard.

CSWE Press
1701 Duke Street, Suite 200
Alexandria, VA 22314-3457
www.cswe.org

Contents

CHAPTER 1

Introduction and Purpose of the Book

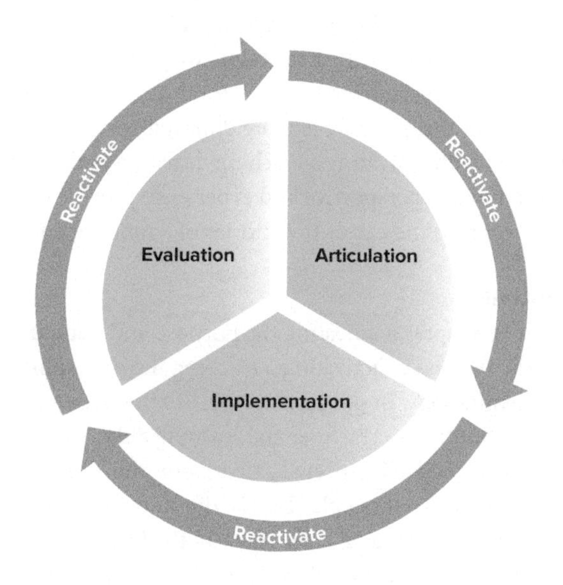

This how-to manual provides a structured framework for developing a comprehensive teaching–learning philosophy from articulation through implementation to evaluation and then, reactivation. Using professional literature and our teaching–learning experiences, we provide pragmatic steps for using a grounded philosophy to inform, engage, and assess teaching and learning. We advocate an integrated teaching–learning philosophy to promote ongoing commitment, engaged competency, and meaningful purpose in our practice as educators.

Although this book provides a substantive resource, its tone is collegial and conversational. As we wrote the book, we drew from the many conversations we have had over the years with each other as coauthors and with other colleagues. These conversations include the countless presenters and authors we have learned from. We imagined sitting with you, the reader, over an informal cup of coffee or in a collegial faculty development seminar in person or online. We intend for this book to serve as the resource we wish we had when we first ventured into the teaching role and, indeed, throughout a career trajectory.

We have been developing the ideas and building blocks for this book for several years. We bring an informed approach and diverse perspectives to this project. We work in varied settings and are at different points in our career development as educators. Jay Miller, teaches at a large, public Research I university; Erlene Grise-Owens taught for more than two decades in small, private university settings; and Larry Owens, teaches on a branch campus of a midsize state university. Likewise, Miller is assistant professor, Grise-Owens achieved tenured full professor rank, and Larry Owens is a tenured associate professor. We have taught in adjunct, visiting, and full-time capacities. Also, we bring a range of practice experience in community and agency roles. In addition, in writing the book, we gleaned input from educators at varying points in their careers, from their doctoral studies to across the span of their careers. Throughout the book, we explore differing perspectives and progress (along with challenges) with activating a teaching–learning philosophy. These complementary variations in perspective and experience provide examples and information that encompass the career trajectories of a range of educators.

Overview of Contents

After this introductory chapter delineating the purpose and structure, the book leads you through the process of activating a teaching–learning philosophy. First, we want to clarify terminology. In our practice, we use the term *teaching–learning philosophy* to convey attention to teaching and learning alike. Congruent with many others (Fox, 2013; hooks, 2003; Roche et al., 1999), our philosophies emphasize that student and faculty are roles, not people. That is, the student and teacher roles are complementary and even interchangeable. Those in the formal faculty role must also be learners, and those in the formal student role must also be teachers. Thus, the teaching–learning process inherently engages all participants in the process of teaching and learning. The literature uses both terms (*teaching philosophy* and *teaching–learning philosophy*). In this book, for brevity, we primarily use teaching philosophy or simply, *philosophy*.

We use the term *activating* to convey the process of taking a teaching philosophy from its conception (i.e., articulation) to putting it into practice (i.e., implementation) and assessing that practice (i.e., evaluation). Then, we emphasize that the philosophy is only meaningful and sustainable through an iterative, intentional reactivation. That is, the implementation and evaluation of a philosophy refines the initial articulation, which then repeats the activation cycle.

We echo Weinstein, Meyer, Husman, Van Mater Stone, and McKeachie's (2006) caution to "be careful not to overemphasize one stage of learning" (p. 282). That is, the essence of the framework in this book is that an activated teaching philosophy is holistic. Activating and reactivating a philosophy requires equal, integrated, and ongoing attention to the facets of articulation, implementation, and evaluation (as shown in the figure on the opening page of this chapter).

In developing this holistic approach, we propose the image of a globe as a metaphor. As we clarify in Chapter 2, a teaching philosophy statement is typically a static product used for a stated purpose (such as a job interview). Thus, as Ratnapradipa and Abrams (2012) said, it can be compared to a road map. However, typically, that road map takes you from Point A (job search) to Point B (job secured), then the map is put aside.

In contrast, having an activated teaching philosophy is a dynamic process, and as such, rather than a road map, is akin to a globe. That is, an activated philosophy is a worldview. Like traveling the globe, an activated philosophy expands your horizons, challenges your perceptions, and deepens your understanding. Ultimately, this approach solidifies connections, enriches your effectiveness, and sustains your professional spirit.

Chapter 2 establishes a theoretical grounding and pragmatic purpose for activating a teaching–learning philosophy. This chapter sets the foundation for understanding how to engage in the process of activation, that is, articulating, implementing, and evaluating and then reactivating. In this chapter, we clarify the important distinction between a teaching philosophy statement (i.e., static product) and an activated philosophy (i.e., dynamic process). This clarification explicates our earlier comparison of the statement as a road map (with limited function) and an activated philosophy as a globe or as an expansive worldview. Then, we emphasize the role of theory in informing an activated philosophy and offer a succinct synthesis of overarching paradigms that can inform theories. From this foundation, we discuss the pragmatic reasons for having a teaching philosophy statement and emphasize using the statement as a starting point for organic activation.

Chapters 3 through 6 guide you through the iterative phases of activating a teaching–learning philosophy. The appendixes of the book contain additional resources, including examples of teaching–learning philosophies, selected resources for writing philosophy statements, and model linkages between professional competencies and a teaching philosophy.

Chapter 3 shows you how to describe and develop a teaching–learning philosophy, using guiding questions such as (a) What do you believe are essential elements for effective teaching–learning? and (b) What is the evidence for these essential elements? This self-reflection and examination toward articulating a teaching philosophy includes the key elements of (a) identifying core values and beliefs about teaching–learning roles and purposes, (b) interpreting inductive experiences in teaching and learning, (c) incorporating the scholarship of teaching and learning (SoTL), and (d) elucidating goodness of fit between teaching philosophy and context, as well as the institutional and personal missions.

Foundational information about this initial phase of articulating a teaching philosophy by writing a philosophy statement is accessible online and from other resources. This chapter provides preliminary examples of resources and instructions on how to find additional resources for writing a teaching philosophy statement. We end Chapter 3 with reflections on our own process of articulating our philosophy. Recognizing the role of stories in the learning process, we offer our different examples to illustrate how to articulate a philosophy.

Next, Chapter 4 describes the implementation phase, how it relates to articulation and evaluation, and the value of this phase. This chapter shows you how to pragmatically link an articulated philosophy with concrete practice. Similar to Chapter 3, this chapter uses guiding questions such as, What in my actual teaching demonstrates or tests my articulated philosophy, that is, which class assignments, classroom activities, syllabus construction, learning environment expectations and norms, and so forth? Practically, this phase involves moving beyond articulating a teaching philosophy to putting the philosophy into praxis. Key elements in this phase include (a) sharing the teaching philosophy with colleagues and students, (b) designing and developing a classroom culture or learning environment that is congruent with the teaching philosophy, (c) identifying specific assignments and activities that demonstrate the teaching philosophy, and (d) selecting modes of assessment congruent with the teaching philosophy.

Chapter 5 provides an array of strategies for linking evaluative components to a teaching philosophy, including formative and ongoing evaluation methods. This chapter focuses on an often-neglected component of the teaching philosophy: evaluation. We discuss four key elements of evaluation (a) valuing evaluation, (b) conceptualizing your evaluation approach, (c) executing your evaluation approach, and (d) responding to and using feedback. This chapter also discusses how this evaluation should be shared with constituents, including students, and how to use this evaluation as material for building a SoTL research agenda. We explain how to pragmatically connect this evaluation to promotion and tenure processes.

In Chapter 6, the book concludes with a discussion about the synergistic effect of continual reactivation of a teaching philosophy statement through attention to the interlocking phases of articulating, implementing, and evaluating. Emphasizing the organic and iterative nature of an activated philosophy, this chapter discusses ways to sustain a teaching–learning philosophy and the benefits of doing so throughout a career. We provide key elements of reactivation, including (a) taking a synergistic approach to the faculty role, (b) fostering a teaching–learning culture, (c) connecting with structural considerations, and (d) sustaining an activated philosophy.

Then we provide our three stories of sustaining our philosophies. Just as we did in Chapter 3, we offer our varied examples to illustrate the importance and impact of an activated philosophy. In our stories, we recount the ways, at various career points, that we sustain a viable philosophy through reactivation. We emphasize the exponential impact that an activated philosophy has in revitalization across a career trajectory. We conclude the book with an invitation for you to activate your philosophy and continue the conversation.

As noted previously, this book is intended as a collegial conversation using an accessible format to provide substantive information and practical strategies. It is an organic resource that educators can continue to use throughout their careers and can be used by any individual faculty member for career development, regardless of the individual's career point. The book is also an ideal text for programs that aim to prepare educators and is an excellent resource for faculty development purposes at the departmental, university, or even broader level. It is a relevant resource that addresses the pertinent need for educators to activate a teaching philosophy.

Here we clarify briefly what this book is not. In our teaching, we strive to offer foundational information, but we focus on teaching students how to critique and apply information and how to think, not just what to think (Brookfield, 2015; Fox, 2013; Paul & Elder, 2004; Weinstein, et al., 1999). This approach prepares students for changing environments by developing adaptable and transferable skills for complex and changing environments (Bean, 2001; Fink, 2003; Lang, 2017; Roche et al., 1999; Vella, 2002).

Similarly, this book does not provide a one-size-fits-all teaching philosophy statement. Rather, it gives you a structure and resources to develop your own activated philosophy much beyond the initial exercise of writing a statement. Also, the book is not a treatise on teaching–learning or educational theories nor on which theories to use. Rather, we discuss the role of theory in activating a philosophy and offer guidance in finding your theoretical base. Finally, this book does not attempt to cover the most recent changes in teaching and learning, such as technological advances and online teaching. Rather, we guide you in developing an activated philosophy that is grounded in core principles but adaptable to emerging information and changing environments. Thus, although informed by current literature, this book provides a framework that can be used across the course of your career.

Why This Book?

Teaching–learning philosophies are increasingly needed to (a) promote an informed and grounded foundation for new educators; (b) provide a framework for educators to use for ongoing development and accountability to various constituents, including accreditors, funders, and public supports; and (c) produce scholarship that informs, documents, and enriches the viable and valuable profession of education (Anastas, 2010; Schönwetter, Sokal, Friesen, & Taylor, 2002; Teater, 2011). Ultimately, an activated philosophy can be an invaluable means of helping seasoned faculty sustain themselves. This resource handbook offers educators ways to enhance skills, knowledge, and values for effective, accountable, and meaningful teaching and learning throughout a career.

Increasingly, statements of teaching philosophy are required for faculty applications and for promotion and tenure reviews (Kearns & Sullivan, 2011; Medina & Draugalis, 2013; Meizlish & Kaplan, 2008; Owens, Miller, & Grise-Owens, 2014). Yet, rarely do faculty have training in how to create teaching philosophies; early career faculty members are often confused about the need for and how to develop a teaching philosophy statement (Clark, 2013; Grundman, 2006; Pryor, 2004; Schussler et al., 2011). If faculty even create philosophy statements, these documents are usually only exercises, in contrast to a purposefully employed document that critically informs teaching and learning in an ongoing fashion.

As Pratt (2005) observed, these initial statements sometimes "make better boxes than ladders" (p. 32). As we noted earlier, these statements are usually products written for a specific task (e.g., job interview) and then packed away in a box or file folder without a real application. In particular, faculty members lack conceptual models and practical guidance for implementing and evaluating a teaching philosophy (Owens, Miller, & Grise-Owens, 2014; Schönwetter et al., 2002). This book encourages you to take your teaching philosophy statement out of the box. Going beyond the box, we encourage you to open up a world of teaching and learning through an expansive globe, namely, an activated philosophy. We guide you through the ongoing iterative process of activating a philosophy across a career.

Increasingly educators face growing demands for accountability, which are linked with myriad factors such as tightening budgetary restraints; changing political climates; increasing knowledge about the brain, cognition, and learning; developing technologies; and growing attention to the realities of diversity in education (Anastas, 2010; Grise-Owens, Owens, & Miller, 2016a). As president of the Carnegie Foundation for the Advancement of Teaching, Boyer (1990) issued a clarion call to education, declaring that education had a "crisis of purpose" (p. 55). He asserted that to remain viable and relevant, educators needed to engage in more creative and accountable processes. This call precipitated the social movement of scholarship of teaching and learning (Hutchings, Huber, & Ciccone, 2011; McKinney, 2013). SoTL can be defined as "active, documented research/inquiry about teaching–learning, which is shared in public forums in order to enrich teaching–learning" (Grise-Owens, Owens, & Miller, 2016, p. 8). The SoTL movement seeks to provide the resources needed to inform, improve, and authenticate the purposes, outcomes, and effectiveness of teaching and learning. An activated philosophy provides a key framework for these aims (Owens, Miller, & Grise-Owens, 2014).

In this context of accountability and engagement, responsible educators see the need for constantly upgrading and maintaining effectiveness. Long-term educators can use an activated philosophy to sustain passion, relevance and career success. This book serves a unique role in providing a guide for promoting meaning, accountability, and effectiveness through the articulation, implementation, and evaluation of one's own practice, that is, teaching and learning.

By extension, this book seeks to promote contributions from educators. Through activating philosophies, educators engage in activities and processes to document our practices and build a teaching commons for best practices (Bishop-Clark & Dietz-Uhler, 2012; Huber & Hutchings, 2005; McKinney, 2012). This documentation can be shared through SoTL forums thus contributing exponentially to the knowledge base. Sustained competence in teaching and learning requires engaged scholarship that critically explores evidence and expands best practices (Grise-Owens, Miller, & Owens, 2016a; Healey, 2003; Huber, 2010; Hutchings, 2010; Weimer, 2006, 2010; Witkin & Saleebey, 2007).

Throughout this book, we synthesize the literature, including our own scholarship as well as our professional experiences. Through this synthesis, we document the importance of a teaching–learning philosophy, as "the foundation by which to clarify goals, to guide behavior, to seed scholarly dialogue on teaching, and to organize evaluation" (Goodyear & Allchin, 1998, p. 103). Further, we provide a framework for developing a meaningful and applicable philosophy (Coppola, 2002; Owens et al., 2014; Pryor, 2004). This book describes how to develop a comprehensive philosophy and seeks to stimulate interest and investment in doing so as engaged scholarship as well as effective practice. We maintain that articulating a teaching–learning philosophy is key yet incomplete. Competent teaching must involve the implementation and evaluation of that philosophy in the classroom and through teaching–learning activities.

How to Use This Book

As stated earlier, we intend for this to be the book we wish we had when we began teaching and as a resource to continue informing and sustaining our professional path. In that spirit, we hope you will use this book in a similar fashion. How you use this resource may vary depending on your individual circumstances, professional role and context, and the point in your career development. The following are some overarching suggestions for how to use the book and are further discussed as we delve more deeply into each phase of articulation, implementation, evaluation, and then reactivation.

First, the book can be used as an individual tool for professional development to guide your process for activating your individual teaching–learning philosophy. It is structured so that an individual faculty member can know how to activate a grounded, organic, and sustainable philosophy. The book can be used from the initial hiring phase through promotion and tenure and for the ongoing sustainment of an engaged career in education.

Second, the book is an ideal text for use in curricula that prepare engaged educators, including but not limited to doctoral programs. Because the book promotes activation of the philosophy beyond the initial articulation, we encourage creating curricula that include ways to build on initial development. In an introductory course on teaching, students can articulate their teaching–learning philosophy and document how they will further implement and evaluate these philosophies. Additional course work throughout the curriculum can build on this initial plan. For example, if the program requires a teaching internship, the students can document during this internship how they activated their teaching philosophy.

Similarly, this book can be used as a resource for ongoing faculty development efforts at the individual unit, university, or broader levels. Mentors can use this book to guide the work with their mentees. It can be a useful resource for faculty development purposes at the department, school, and university levels, as well as in broader educator training venues. The book can be used to inform unit- and university-level activation of a jointly shared philosophical approach. As such, the book can support accountability efforts, such as institutional effectiveness and accreditation.

Emphatically, we intend for this book to serve an organic and adaptable purpose. Teaching–learning philosophies and their activation have unique and universal aspects. That is, a teaching–learning philosophy is a personal endeavor; your individual philosophy must reflect the uniqueness of who you are and what you bring to the educational experience. Similarly, if treated with purpose and passion, your philosophy is not a stagnant document. Rather, it will evolve as you move through your career trajectory.

At the same time, many universal aspects apply in activating a teaching–learning philosophy. This book discusses those universal dimensions in a manner that provides pragmatic guidance for faculty throughout their career path and that can inform the use of teaching–learning philosophies for broader units, such as a shared departmental philosophy. Concomitantly, the book allows your unique exploration and activation. These universal and unique aspects will inform, document, and sustain an organic, effective, and meaningful teaching–learning philosophy and, by extension, the broader field of education. So, let's get activated! ■

Chapter 2

What Is a Teaching Philosophy and Why Do I Need One?

Some of you may have articulated a philosophy in a concrete way; others are operating from a philosophy even though it may be unconscious. Whether or not you have a product (e.g., a written statement), you have certain beliefs and values about teaching and learning that you incorporate into your work or that guide your conception of teaching and learning. Depending on where you are in conceptualizing your philosophy, you may experience incongruence in your work because some of those values and perspectives are not consistently implemented in your teaching–learning practice. This unconsciousness and incongruence can cause particular frustration and confusion for educators. Effective teaching and learning requires an activated philosophy.

This chapter sets the foundation for understanding how to engage in the process of activation, that is, articulating, implementing, evaluating, and then reactivating. In this chapter, we clarify the important distinction between a teaching philosophy statement (i.e., static product) and an activated philosophy (i.e., dynamic process). This clarification expands on our earlier comparison of the statement as a road map, with limited function, and an activated philosophy as a globe, or an expansive worldview. This distinction leads to emphasizing the value of ongoing critical reflection. We emphasize the role of theory in informing an activated philosophy and offer a succinct synthesis of overarching paradigms that can inform theories. From this foundation, we discuss the pragmatic reasons for having a teaching philosophy statement and emphasize using the statement as a starting point for organic activation.

Distinguishing Product From Process

Much of the literature associated with teaching philosophies or statements has focused on the activity of writing down the teaching philosophy statement. The literature is replete with frameworks and exercises associated with this task, and scores of online resources are available for designing teaching statements (see Appendix A). Yet, challenges and misnomers persist. In fact, for some, the prospect of having to write a teaching statement, no matter the reason, is maligned. In one of the prominent works about teaching philosophies, Chism (1998) described the process of writing a teaching philosophy statement as "irritating" (p. 1). This irritation may be attributed, at least in part, to the lack of engaged, conceptual thinking through of one's philosophy.

Against this backdrop, it is imperative to draw a distinction between a teaching philosophy and a teaching philosophy statement. These terms are often used interchangeably in the educational nomenclature. Occasionally the term *teaching portfolio* even becomes confused with these terms. Understanding the difference will help you more adeptly conceptualize the framework for building your philosophy and your statement. Simply put, clarity comes in distinguishing between product and process. To clarify, a teaching portfolio is typically the written product presented in a promotion and tenure process to document your teaching. The portfolio contains your teaching statement (product). Notably, in the digital era, that product can be produced and distributed electronically and may include written text, images, audio, and video to convey the philosophy. If constructed in a meaningful and organic fashion, the portfolio contains evidence or your activated philosophy (process). This process can be enlivened through the use of interactive multimedia platforms to update and share the ongoing activation of your teaching philosophy.

The initial and ongoing development of your activated philosophy requires critical analyses of your thoughts about how people teach and learn, and the juxtaposition of the two. Further, you must consider contextual factors that may affect your analyses: What are the institutional norms and mores where you teach? What are the expectations? How are these ideals communicated? Likewise, you must critically and conscientiously traverse broader considerations, such as how teaching and learning occurs in a rapidly changing, culturally diverse environment. Education is affected by consumerism, expected to produce global citizens, and faced with changing political climates. How do you navigate the challenges and opportunities of these considerations?

In the upcoming chapters the core of developing and activating your teaching philosophy is ongoing critical reflection about the known and unknown, what you have experienced and what you have not, educational environments, and so forth. The influential works of Dewey (1938), Schön (1983), Schmier (1995), and others discussed the importance of critical reflection in education. Much of this reflection assuredly revolves around exploring your own experiences as a student and educator. Pragmatically, through all this exploration and reflection, you are provided with the opportunity to step back from focusing solely on your field of study and instead consider thoughts and beliefs about teaching and learning more broadly.

The Role of Theory in an Activated Philosophy

Although a teaching philosophy is highly personal, adeptly developing one also requires substantive interaction with, and critical reflection about, educational scholarship (i.e., SoTL). A more expansive discussion about engagement in SoTL, and its crucial role, is integrated throughout the book. In addition, an activated philosophy requires critical understanding of foundational educational theory. Yes, *theory*.

To clarify, as a how-to resource, this book is not a treatise on the role of theory associated with teaching philosophies. However, theory should play a role in developing your teaching philosophy. Your philosophy ought to be grounded in or at least informed by theory. As an educator, you may encourage your students to think about the philosophical underpinnings of particular perspectives, practices, or approaches. Similarly, as a component of thinking about and defining your philosophy, we encourage the exploration of applicable theories that inform, confirm, and challenge your beliefs about teaching and learning (Teater, 2011). In so doing, you connect your philosophy to an existing knowledge base, which inherently helps give your philosophy some legitimacy and credibility. This connection refines your philosophy in an iterative fashion. The following discussion briefly explains the important role that theory plays in helping reactivate a philosophy.

Theories seek to explain. Traditionally, these explanations are grounded in some framework based on a pattern of observed behaviors or circumstances, and from this pattern, we can assume something will happen, some phenomena will occur, and so forth (Schön, 1983). Thus, educational theory seeks to explain how individuals teach and learn (Merriman, 2001). In turn, these theories, at least ideally, inform how we educate.

Historically, educational theory "has seldom been a popular subject" among new or seasoned educators (Moore, 2012, p. 1), yet the thought that educational theory is superfluous endures. In fact, many educators do not have adequate knowledge of or a relevant background in educational theory (Coppolla, 2002). Even educators who are erudite in theories can find that the application of theory can lead to what Burghardt (2016) described as theory clashing, that is, tension between a theory and practical application of the theory or even differences among theories. These dynamics have affected the way we think, or not, about applying educational theory to the construction of teaching philosophies (Beatty, Leigh, & Dean, 2009b; Ratnapradipa & Abrams, 2012), which has led many philosophies to be "undertheorized" (Alexander et al., 2012, p. 23).

Reams have been written on educational and pedagogical theories. Here we provide a succinct summary of some salient points to provide a foundational understanding for you to pursue in activating your own philosophy. In essence, these theories can fall under three overarching paradigms: behaviorism, cognitivism, and constructivism (Ertmer & Newby, 1993). Under each of these overarching paradigms, myriad theories have evolved.

We want to emphasize an essential point. This brief summary of prevalent literature is not comprehensive; inherently, it privileges particular perspectives. However, this summary gives you a basic foundation. Evolving theories continue to critique, challenge, and modify these privileged paradigms. In activating your philosophy, it will be essential for you to explore these expansive theories.

In these overarching paradigms, several authors have distinguished between teaching theories and learning theories. Knowles, Holton, and Swanson (2005) explained that theories about learning seek to explain how individuals learn; theories about teaching seek to explain how a teacher affects an individual's learning. Others have made similar distinctions (Driscoll, 2004; Reigeluth, 1983). Although this distinction is helpful in organizing and examining theories, teaching and learning theories are connected and mutually informative (Caulfield, 2011). Thus, teaching and learning theories should be used to inform the development of your philosophy.

We don't intend to provide a laundry list of theories that may or may not be applicable to conceptualizing your teaching philosophy. Extensive works have been produced that are exclusively devoted to discussing theories of teaching and learning, and many books have been wholly devoted to examining these works. Weimer (2002) provided an "eclectic reading list" (p. 228) associated with pedagogical and andragogical paradigms and theories; we recommend perusing this list.

However, we do think it is necessary to provide some foundational information related to some of the more prominently (in terms of literature) recognized educational worldviews. Driscoll (2004) offered an excellent and comprehensive work for examining these theoretical approaches more deeply. For instance, although often criticized for the overemphasis on observed behavior (e.g., Driscoll), behaviorism (Skinner, 1953, 1954, 1974; Watson, 1928, 1930) has been influential in conceptualizing the way that educators think about teaching and learning. In the behaviorism canon, educators view students as docile beings who are influenced by reinforcement, whether positive or negative. Pragmatically, this approach may be best demonstrated in the following scenario: Student writes a paper, student receives a good grade (positive reinforcement), student learns that elements of the paper are good, and student seeks to mimic the paper in the future.

Cognitivism and constructivism also help to provide some organizational clarity of teaching–learning theories. The former focuses, as the name implies, on the cognitive ability of the learner to take in and process information as a mechanism for learning. Gagne's (1962, 1985, 1987) work, some of which is rooted in some of the primary tenets of behaviorism (Driscoll, 2004), is an example of cognitivism. This theoretical framework primarily focuses on an individual's intellectual capacity. In essence, Gagne's theoretical work has centered on three areas: learning outcomes, conditions suitable for meeting learning outcomes, and instructional approaches (e.g., Gagne, Briggs, Wager, 1992; Gagne & Driscoll, 1988). Much of the well-known work related to Bloom's taxonomy (Bloom, Engelhart, Furst, Hill, & Krathwohl, 1956) was influenced by the work of Gagne. Notably, Bloom's taxonomy has been refined since initial inception (Krathwohl, 2002). Piaget (1970) is also a well-known theorist associated with cognitive approaches.

In constructivism, and for those who subscribe to this school of thought, learning is viewed as a dynamic process that focuses on contributing to the construction of knowledge rather than just consuming knowledge. According to Belenky and Stanton (2000), individuals who adhere to this school of thought understand that "knowledge is constructed by the mind, not by procedures" (p. 90). In this canon, knowledge is viewed as a constructed process, not an end product. Ultimately, this approach considers experiences and reflections as integral parts of the teaching–learning processes.

Several educational philosophers and theorists have contributed works that fall into this category. Perhaps most notably, are those from Dewey (1910, 1934). These works, as well as others, have examined the importance of problem solving, and the resulting experiences, as an instructional avenue in which individuals learn. Vygotsky's (1978) active learning theory examines the role that meaning plays in how a learner constructs understanding and knowing.

A host of other perspectives may offer theoretical insight into developing your philosophy. For instance, Bandura's (1977) social cognitive theory asserted that educational outcomes are affected by personal attributes, behavior, and contextual (e.g., environmental) factors. Kolb's (1981, 1984) learning theory views learning as a reciprocal process in which new experiences form the context for new learning. Similarly, Mezirow's (1978, 1990, 2003) transformative learning theory examined the role of experience in learning. Mitzel's (1960) theory on teaching and learning was predicated on relationships among presage, context, process, and product variables.

Criticalist theory explicitly considers the role of power in the learning process, particularly the hegemonic, marginalizing impact of privilege and the need to access multiple standpoints in the educational process (Freire, 2000; Graham, 1997; Saleebey & Scanlon, 2005) Criticalist theory critiques traditional, positivistic educational paradigms. Criticalists contend that traditional educational approaches "marginalize students by failing to recognize and develop their [power], while also oppressing educators by disallowing them to bring their whole selves to their work" (Pyles & Adam, 2016, p. 7).

These theories, and myriad other theories, perspectives, and critiques, will play out in multiple ways as you begin to think about your philosophy. For example, in his philosophy, coauthor Jay Miller encapsulates a constructivist approach and criticalist pedagogy, rooted in transformative and active learning theories, among others. Congruent with facets of these theories, Jay views individuals in the roles of educator and student as interdependent co-learners, all of whom have a responsibility in co-constructing knowledge. Actually, all three of our philosophies are significantly informed by complementary theories that stem from a constructivist paradigm and critical theory. For example, we all are attuned to the impact and interplay of diversity, power, privilege, and marginalization in the educational experience. Our philosophies implicitly and explicitly address those considerations. Happily, these complementary theories are synthesized in writings that have been pivotal in guiding the activation of our philosophies as situated in social work education (Fox, 2013; Graham, 1997; Pyles & Adam, 2016; Roche et al., 1999; Saleebey & Scanlon, 2005; Witkin & Saleebey, 2007). As we explain in the next chapter, drawing from this wealth of the theoretical knowledge base will significantly inform and shape organic activation of your philosophy.

First, the Statement: What Is a Teaching Philosophy Statement?

As you continue to develop and refine your teaching philosophy, you will begin to actualize your philosophy by writing down a teaching philosophy statement. Your statement is the mechanism for communicating your philosophy. Said another way, the statement is an enunciated philosophy, a product that logically connects your philosophy to actionable measures.

Schönwetter et al. (2002) described the philosophy statement as "a systematic and critical rationale that focuses on the important components defining effective teaching and learning in a particular discipline and/or institutional context" (p. 84). Your teaching philosophy statement should provide direction for classroom decorum, instructional approaches, and learning outcomes (Light & Cox, 2001). In essence, your statement should communicate your values as an educator and state the purpose of your teaching (Crookes, 2009; Felicilda-Reynaldo, & Utley, 2015; Fitzmaurice, 2008; Glaser, 2008; Licklider, 2004; Stamm, 1997).

As Schönwetter et al. (2002) suggested, putting the statement into words is a decidedly personal endeavor. Like cultivating your philosophy, drafting the statement requires deep critical reflection. Coppola (2002) described writing the statement as the "cornerstone of reflective and scholarly practice in teaching–learning" (p. 448). At its core, your statement reflects your beliefs and thoughts about teaching, learning, and instructional methods (Grundman, 2006).

There is no consensus on the exact format and structure of a teaching philosophy statement. Further, the process of writing a teaching statement is a relatively new endeavor. Consequently, educators are often hesitant about crafting a statement (Seldin, 1991). Additionally, as Seldin observed, educators may avoid creating a teaching statement out of concern about what they might discover.

Lack of consensus notwithstanding, a number of scholars have offered guidance on composing a philosophy statement. Generally, a teaching philosophy statement includes at least four focus areas: conceptualization of how learning occurs, conceptualization of an effective teaching and learning environment, expectations of the student-teacher relationship, and student assessment and assessment of learning goals (Coppola, 2002; Eierman, 2008: Goodyear & Allchin, 1998; Grundman, 2006;

Kearns & Sullivan, 2011; O'Neil, Meizlish, & Kaplan, 2007; Schönwetter et al., 2002). Chism (1998) recommended that a teaching philosophy should be written in the first person, and Eierman (2008) contended that statements should include references.

In addition to these four general foci of a teaching philosophy statement, Chism (1998) recommended a personal growth plan, and Eierman (2008) included teaching interests and references. Goodyear and Allchin (1998) stressed the integration of teaching, scholarship, and service into the teaching philosophy statement. Also, the use of metaphor can be effective in illustrating aspects of the educator's teaching philosophy (Bulik & Shokar, 2007; Chism, 1998; Coppola, 2002; Schönwetter, et al., 2002). Beatty et al. (2009a) provided a practical step-by-step facilitator's guide to formulating a teaching philosophy statement. They suggested the use of guided imagery and a card-sorting exercise that links what the teacher believes about teaching with prominent educational theories.

Some authors, such as Grundman (2006), emphasized that the teaching philosophy statement should be student-centered. We contend that the teaching philosophy statement should be learning centered, which addresses the current problematic trend of viewing students as consumers (Fox, 2013; Miller & Owens, 2008). This reframing allows a broader examination of the classroom as a learning environment in which students and teachers actively contribute to teaching–learning environments. This approach more explicitly considers diversity, power, privilege, and marginalization, and how to engage those considerations to enhance meaningful, deep learning (Owens et al., 2014).

In addition, as with many aspects of the academic role (Gutierrez, 2012; Wilson, Valentine, & Pereira, 2002), mentorship can be helpful in producing a statement. Kearns and Sullivan (2011) stressed the importance of faculty mentoring, particularly for graduate and postdoctoral students and recommended a five-paragraph essay teaching philosophy model that incorporates learning goals, teaching methods, learning assessment, and teaching assessment. They synthesized several other teaching statement models, such as the teaching cube (Duquesne University, n.d.) and a self-reflective interview exercise (Ellis & Griffin, 2000). Kaplan, et al. (2007) offered a rubric for developing a teaching statement.

Although a general framework is provided in the literature, we emphasize that the process of crafting a teaching philosophy statement is varied and personal. All in all, "the teaching philosophy statement can be crafted in whatever form best communicates the applicant's beliefs and strengths" (Grundman, 2006, p. 1392).

Why Do I Need a Teaching Philosophy Statement and Activated Philosophy?

Interested in applying for a job in the academy? Taking part in an annual evaluation? Up for a teaching award? Want to be promoted, dare we say, earn tenure? If so, chances are that you will be required to have a teaching philosophy statement (Chism, 1998; Eierman, 2008; Owens et al., 2014).

Delineating a clear conception related to teaching, that is, a teaching philosophy, serves several functions. Fundamentally, the philosophy statement and its activation will provide a framework for how you engage in teaching and learning. The teaching philosophy statement and activated philosophy serves other utilitarian functions. For instance, many students making the transition into academe as an educator will likely be required to submit a teaching philosophy statement as part of a professional dossier. The majority of openings for academic positions require the submission of a teaching philosophy statement (Eierman, 2008). In today's competitive academic marketplace, one would be hard pressed to find an open position that does not have such a requirement. Eierman suggested that these philosophies and statements may be used to assess an applicant's commitment to teaching and the knowledge of teaching–learning approaches. Anastas (2010) declared that a teaching philosophy, even if not required, shows that an educator views teaching as a "deliberate, professional, and self-reflective activity" (p. 57). Thus, the teaching philosophy statement is an integral component of obtaining positions in academe.

Not only is the teaching philosophy statement pertinent to obtaining a job, it is also important to maintaining a job. If you are already employed as an educator, chances are you will be (or have been) required to submit a statement for promotion and tenure processes (Meizlish & Kaplan, 2008; Pratt, 2005). In addition to promotion and tenure reviews, teaching statements may also be used for evaluative purposes, particularly for lecturers, clinical faculty, or other non-tenure-seeking appointments with teaching responsibilities. Many doctoral students may be tasked with developing a teaching philosophy statement as part of a course requirement. In many of these instances, a teaching statement can be used to identify strengths and weaknesses associated with teaching–learning activities (Ratnapradipa & Abrams, 2012). Statements can be an effective way to communicate teaching–learning approaches to students (see Chapter 3).

Now, Let's Activate a Teaching Philosophy

As you read this book, we guide you through a framework to take the teaching philosophy statement from a static product to an activated philosophy. As we said in Chapter 1: Think of a teaching philosophy statement as a road map, typically used for a one-time purpose, such as getting from Point A (job interview) to Point B (a job). In contrast, an activated philosophy is akin to a globe in that an activated philosophy expands your worldview. A teaching philosophy statement, without activation, is a static product. If you do not go beyond this initial road map, you risk being stuck on the same road. Typically, over time this road becomes rutted by routine. Thus, your teaching can become rote, and your professional spirit become stagnant. But if you decide to activate a philosophy, it will expand your horizons. This expansive worldview, your activated teaching philosophy, will sustain your teaching spirit and generate synergistic learning experiences.

Here are some reminders as we begin that activation. First, as we discussed at the beginning of this chapter, simply not having a statement does not mean that you do not have a philosophy (Coppolla, 2002). Every educator has a set of guiding principles, written, articulated, or otherwise, that guide what they do and how they do it. Your philosophy is omnipresent. Jaspers (1951) described this notion as follows: "There is no escape from philosophy. The question is only whether a philosophy is conscious or not, whether it is good or bad, muddled or clear. Anyone who rejects philosophy is himself [*sic*] unconsciously practicing a philosophy" (p. 12). In the framework we present in the following chapters, the teaching statement is the distillation of the articulated philosophy.

Second, your teaching statement and philosophy are mutually informing. As you continue reading this book, you may start to view the process, or the phases for activating your teaching philosophy, as wholly linear. But this perspective does not capture the integrated complexity of developing your philosophy, which is articulated in your statement and activated through an iterative process. Beatty et al. (2009b) argued that the process of developing a teaching philosophy is as important as the content of the product, which is the statement. This process is dynamic. The philosophy informs the statement, which if actualized, provides a mechanism to continuously evaluate the philosophy, which in turn refines a statement about that philosophy.

This observation brings us to a third point: Your philosophy is organic. Congruent with notions shared by Schön (1987), Giroux (1988), and others, educators teach in contexts that are ever changing. In his discussion of his own evolution, award-winning author Stephen Brookfield (2015) said that his ongoing "journey as a teacher through diverse contexts and irresolvable dilemmas is bound to generate new insights" (p. 276). Indeed, through exchanges that occur in a learning community, students as well as teachers are changed (Freire, 1998a, b). At any given point in time, your philosophy is a philosophy, not the philosophy. Thus, your teaching philosophy must continuously evolve to meet the learning outcomes and values it strives to reflect (Reber, 2011).

A philosophy and statement are not something that you get right and certainly are not an end. Every class you teach, lecture you give, syllabus you design, learning activity you facilitate, and student you interact with will indubitably shape your perspective. Use these opportunities to refine, energize, and sustain your philosophy. In the following chapters, we talk about how to use every aspect of your teaching–learning life to activate an effective and viable philosophy. No boring boxes or rutted road maps for us. Bring on the globe of activation! ■

Chapter 3

How Do I Articulate My Philosophy?

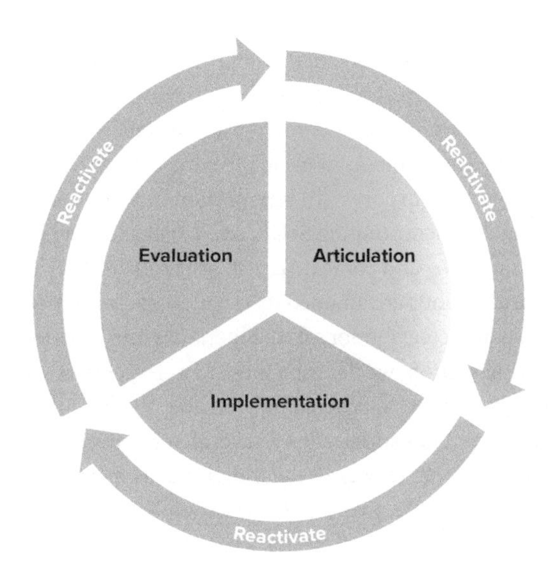

As mentioned earlier, the articulation phase receives the most attention in the literature and in practice. Developing and submitting a teaching philosophy statement is a common component of the application process for academic positions. A well-articulated teaching philosophy statement provides academic search committees with an insight into an applicant's core beliefs and values about the learning process. The teaching philosophy statement explains the approach to facilitating learning in and outside the classroom (Medina & Draugalis, 2013; Peters, 2009; Pryor, 2004; Schussler et al., 2011). As we clarified in Chapter 2, the teaching philosophy statement is a product, whereas an activated philosophy is an engaged process.

However, for many aspiring academics and educators, developing a teaching philosophy statement is rarely considered anything more than one of the necessary steps to secure an academic position (Alexander et al., 2011; Beatty et al., 2009b). Often, new educators strive to develop a teaching philosophy statement that is generic enough to meet the wide range of possible expectations of search committees while also reflecting their specific values, beliefs, and approach to teaching. In other words, the goal for the teaching philosophy statement is limited to meeting expectations without hurting one's chances for securing the academic position. As such, it becomes an abstract exercise with limited usefulness.

We advocate that developing a teaching philosophy statement should and can be so much more than just another rote exercise in securing a job. Emphatically, the value of developing a meaningful teaching philosophy lies not just in a final product, the statement. More so, we agree with Beatty et al. (2009a) that the sustainable value lies in the process, which is activating the philosophy. In this frame, articulating a teaching philosophy requires self-reflection and examination of what you bring to the teaching–learning process. This articulation provides an essential foundation for building a meaningful, effective, and sustainable career in academia.

Thus, this self-reflection and examination toward articulating a teaching philosophy includes the key elements of (a) identifying core values and beliefs about teaching–learning roles and purposes, (b) interpreting inductive experiences in teaching and learning, (c) incorporating SoTL, and (d) elucidating goodness of fit between teaching philosophy and context, as well as the institutional and personal missions. These considerations are attained through critical reflection as well as engaged participation and contributions to the literature and broader scholarship (i.e., SoTL). In the following section, we describe these key elements of articulation then share some of the steps we used in articulating our own teaching–learning philosophy.

We reiterate: Teaching philosophies have several key universal facets, which we discuss throughout this book. However, the individual aspects make an activated philosophy most viable and effective, and these examples will certainly provide ideas for how to better articulate your philosophy. We stress that the teaching philosophy should be personal and unique and specific enough to be meaningful to you individually. Concomitantly, it needs to be broad enough to be malleable as you grow in the profession. The philosophy is organic in that it is reactivated over time through the iterative process of articulation, implementation, and evaluation. In this chapter, we illustrate this organicity by alluding to examples of how we have sharpened the articulation of our teaching philosophies over time while retaining the original facets of articulation. Chapter 6 delves more deeply into this reactivation over the trajectory of a career.

Identifying Core Values and Beliefs

An initial step in articulating a teaching philosophy statement involves identifying your core values and beliefs about the functions, facets, processes, purposes, roles, and goals of education. Weimer (2010) observed that most teachers don't have a good grasp of their own teaching "in intimate and detailed ways … [as] a result of little or no training about how to teach [and] not being terribly reflective about what we do when we teach." (p. 23). As McCormick and Kennelly (2011) asserted, reflection is needed that involves "intense scrutiny of conceptions, values, and principles of [your] teaching" (p. 526).

Fink (2003) summarized the four major components of teaching as teacher-student interactions, knowledge of subject matter, design of instruction, and course management. Articulating a teaching philosophy involves considering what you believe and value about these components. This step considers questions such as the following:

- What is the role of the educator?
- What is the role of student?
- How does the student or learner, teacher, and the environment interact or relate?
- What should the teaching–learning environment be like?
- What is knowledge and truth?
- What are the functions and goals of education?
- How should I design and manage or facilitate the teaching–learning process?
- How does my teaching style and substance have an impact on learning?

Identifying core values and beliefs involves looking at your views of humankind as a whole. A meaningful philosophy statement must articulate your values and beliefs about the interaction among individuals. Teaching and learning involves interaction with others, and it is key for you to articulate your values concerning that interaction. For example, if one of your core values is a belief in egalitarianism and equality, that belief will have an impact on your interaction with students and colleagues and how you view the learning environment. Thus, as you articulate your teaching philosophy, it is imperative for you to know and understand the core values that influence who you are as an individual and how you view your connection with others.

In a broader sense, this reflection considers what you believe about knowledge and truth and the roles of the teacher and learner in relation to the construction of knowledge. Further, the reflective articulation considers what you believe and value about the classroom environment, structure of learning, and your role in it. For instance, is knowledge co-constructed? Does the teacher facilitate learning or dispense truth? Is the student a passive recipient or active participant? Again, we recommend giving explicit attention to power, privilege, marginalization, and diversity in reflecting on all these questions. These dynamics affect every aspect of the educational experience.

A related consideration is how do you balance disclosure of personal identities and experiences through an activated teaching philosophy especially when those identities and experiences are integrally tied to your approach to teaching and learning? That is, how much of your *self* do you share? How do you balance professional boundaries with human connection in the learning experience?

As we discuss later, we try to be transparent about power dynamics, diverse positionalities, and their impact on the educational experience. Oftentimes this transparency involves modeling. For instance, we acknowledge the privilege embedded in dominant social identities as well as the oppression inherent in marginalized identities for everyone in the educational experience. Likewise, we connect our teaching philosophy approaches to these understandings. For instance, we emphasize the need for everyone to contribute to the teaching–learning process thus expanding the co-construction of knowledge beyond the privileged perspectives. We set parameters for these spaces to "liberate the voices of all participants" (Dean, 2007, p. 43).

In considering this aspect of your teaching philosophy, we recommend delving into the literature about attention to social and personal identities in the educational experience. Also, consider role models in your circle and in the literature. For instance, in their prolific writings, Freire, hooks, and Palmer, among others, model and discuss this aspect in all their works (see reference list). In addition, we recommend reading autoethnographic narratives and reflecting on how others' experiences may inform your own approach. For instance, Lay (2005) reflects on how being *out* in her professional role stems from her teaching philosophy's value of transparency:

> I am a lesbian who is 'out' in the classroom. There is no event, such as an announcement: I simply am fully me. ... Being out in the classroom ... [invites] the learner to acknowledge presence, understanding, and inclusion of others." (p. 20)

Grise-Owens and Lay (2009) include several narratives from faculty on how they integrate a range of personal identities and professional roles while ensuring healthy boundaries.

This examination of your values and beliefs seeks to get at the core of who you are individually and your connection with those around you as demonstrated in your role as educator. This examination is a personal reflection that grows from your knowledge and experiences initially. This reflection encompasses not only your current values and beliefs but also the person and educator you are striving to become (Beatty et al., 2009a; Graham, 1997; Palmer, 2013; Peters & Weisberg, 2011; Sankey & Foster, 2012; Schussler et al., 2011; Weisenberg & Stacey, 2005; Weimer, 2010).

The following are some additional resources to inform your ongoing process of reflection. McGranahan's (2008) self-reflection on her first year of teaching concluded with a critical and constructive list titled "What I Would Do Differently" (pp. 33–34). Her reflection provides an accessible and explicit example of the necessary process for articulating a teaching philosophy. Reflecting on the trajectory of her teaching career, Grise-Owens (2011) articulated her teaching philosophy through the lens of spirituality with practical applications. Palmer's (e.g., 1998) extensive work is widely recognized as offering reflection and pragmatic pointers for educators. Another prominent influence, hooks (1994, 2003) reflected on and reconstructed pedagogy through a critical lens. Likewise, Freire's (1998) reflective book crystalized his iconic work. Ada (2007) offered a complementary perspective to McGranahan's first year, reflecting beautifully on what she learned in a "lifetime of learning to teach." (p. 103). Similarly, Parini (2005) offered a model for reflecting on the trajectory of a career in teaching. Brookfield's (1995) classic book is another recommended resource. Peters and Weisberg (2011) published an excellent reflection workbook to guide the articulation of your philosophy and ongoing activation.

Notably, much of this reflection will be a solitary endeavor; ultimately, you alone decide what your philosophy is. However, we highly recommend pursuing collaborative processes for this reflection. For example, any of the resources listed here can be used for reflective discussion with colleagues whether in a reading or book club format, faculty development workshop, or just informal chats. Certainly, this book can be used as a guide for such reflective conversations. McCormick and Kennelly (2011) studied three "conversation communities" (p. 515) in which faculty reflected together for a period of time so that each member of the communities could write a teaching philosophy. (See Chapter 6 for a more extensive discussion of the use of learning communities.) Participants in McCormick and Kennelly's study reported positive effects of these reflective conversations with colleagues and found that connection, engagement, and safety were key factors in this success.

Interpreting Inductive Experiences

As stated earlier, articulating a philosophy requires identifying core values and beliefs through critical reflection. Concomitantly, articulating your philosophy requires reflecting on your own experiences as a learner and teacher alike. You have experience with teaching and learning through your own educational process. You have been (or are) a student. You had teachers who inspired and challenged you. Regrettably, you likely encountered instructors whom you found boring, were unable to connect with, or you had other negative experiences with. You likely have thought, "If I were teaching this class, I would—" We would venture to say that because you are considering a career in education, or are in the midst of one, your experience has been more positive than negative. As we emphasized in Chapter 2, you have already formed a philosophy of sorts, or at least initial ideas, based on those experiences

Undoubtedly, your values and beliefs about teaching and learning are implicitly affected by your own experience with education. Your experience needs to be critically explored in a reflective process to make it explicit. Some of the critical questions to consider include the following:

- What did you find effective in your own learning when you were in the student role? How did you see teachers adapt their approach for different learning styles?

- When do you experience moments of deep, meaningful learning and teaching both as a student as well as teacher?
- How do your core values connect with your experiences?
- What dissonance do you experience between your values and experiences?
- In many instances, it will be important to consider the congruence between the values of your chosen discipline and your teaching. How do your core values and the values of your chosen discipline (e.g., history, social work, nursing, engineering) show through in your teaching philosophy?

Similarly, your philosophy should be informed by your life experiences and professional background. Earlier, we discussed the importance of reflecting on how much of your personal and social identities you disclose in your teaching. As we illustrate in our following examples, you want to acknowledge and connect your philosophy to the unique aspects you bring to the teaching role. In this sense, your personal experiences and perspective will be evident in style and substance. For example, as elaborated on later, Erlene's *word nerdiness* is evident in her alliterative philosophy, Larry's love of travel comes through in his philosophy, and Jay's dedication to service and demonstrating through action (e.g., modeling behaviors) profoundly affects his philosophy.

One way to capture a teaching philosophy is through metaphors, which can encapsulate the meaning of your philosophy and provide a construct for developing the philosophy (Bulik & Shokar, 2007; Schönwetter, et al., 2002; Roche et al., 2009). Fox (2013) has an excellent chapter on metaphors of teaching, and Fink (2003) uses the metaphor of a *helmsman* [sic] throughout her book as a depiction of the role of teacher.

However, other faculty opt for other approaches in conveying their philosophy. Metaphor is one commonly used formula, not *the* formula. Again, embrace your own style.

Incorporating SoTL

Although staying true to your unique style, your philosophy must be informed by more universally tested educational theories and best practices. In Chapter 2, we discussed the role of theory and synthesized theoretical paradigms. In addition to this attention to theory, an activated philosophy relies on ongoing attention to best practices.

Thus, an essential element in the articulation of a teaching philosophy is Scholarship of Teaching–Learning (SoTL). A term coined by Boyer (1990), SoTL involves research designed to investigate effective teaching and learning. Boyer, and others who have built on his work, contended that SoTL is an essential arena of scholarship for responsible educators. SoTL is purposeful, reflective, documented, and shared in public evaluative forums, which contribute to the knowledge base (Shulman, 2000; Wang, 2012; Weimer, 2010. In essence, SoTL is active learning about teaching, which is shared with others with the intent of enriching teaching and learning (Grise-Owens, Owens, & Miller, 2016a).

Please, realize that a whole world of resources await in the arena of SoTL. The

SoTL movement is a vibrant and valuable forum, which is growing in impact and importance (Gurung & Schwartz, 2010; Healy, 2003; Huber, 2010; Huber & Hutchings, 2005; Shulman, 2004; Wehbi, 2009). When we began participating in SoTL through literature, workshops, and conferences, we discovered resources that resonated with and challenged our initial teaching–learning philosophy that we had articulated inductively through our experiences. Then, as we began contributing to SoTL through our own scholarship, our teaching and learning became even more viable and meaningful.

Just as any quality research includes a review of the literature, the articulation of a meaningful teaching philosophy statement includes grounding from the knowledge base about teaching and learning. SoTL provides that knowledge base. Thus, a familiarity with basic learning theory gives you a foundation in building your philosophy statement, and a review of pertinent SoTL material introduces you to strategies, techniques, and an understanding of what works (and doesn't work) in the learning environment. Further, a review of SoTL gives more legitimacy and strength to the assertions made in your teaching philosophy statement. SoTL is where you test your individual introspection through considering the broader knowledge base about teaching–learning theories and best practices.

We provide a few resources to help you develop SoTL as an essential aspect of activating your teaching philosophy. We believe so strongly in the importance of SoTL that we contributed an invited article on the topic for the *Journal of Social Work Education.* Grise-Owens, Owens, & Miller (2016a) gives a brief history and rationale of SoTL then it provides a succinct step-by-step guide to help you build your SoTL agenda. The article discusses how to pursue a SoTL agenda for research even in contexts that may not initially place value on that line of research. The article also provides additional resources, for example, literature and avenues such as teaching conferences.

Among the many resources available, Bishop-Clark & Dietz-Uhler (2012) provide a useful workbook for developing a SoTL project from inception to completion. Werder & Otis (2010) provide an important resource for developing SoTL that engages students as collaborators. Among her extensive, excellent contributions on SoTL, McKinney's (2013) edited book on interdisciplinary SoTL is a synthesizing resource. Finally, as another prolific contributor to SoTL (though she uses the term *pedagogical scholarship*), Weimer's (2006) book offers a comprehensive and accessible summary of interdisciplinary SoTL.

In addition, we recommend you access other printed resources and conference materials. Weimer et al. founded an annual conference, blog, and newsletter titled *The Teaching Professor*, which are excellent resources (www.magnapubs.com/newsletter/the-teaching-professor/index.html). Similarly, the Lilly Conference Series on College and University Teaching and Learning annually hosts an international conference as well as several regional conferences in the United States (lillyconferences.com). The Wakonse Conference on College Teaching (http://

wakonse.org) each summer sponsors an interdisciplinary conference on teaching, which we experienced more like a refreshing summer camp for professors. The International Higher Education Teaching and Learning Association hosts an international conference annually (https://www.hetl.org), and the International Society for the Scholarship of Teaching and Learning (https://www.issotl.com/) holds annual conferences in different locations. These organizations have other resources, such as journals, newsletters, and blogs.

It is likely that your discipline has a conference and other related resources specifically focused on teaching with technology. A growing number of interdisciplinary resources for teaching with technology include Quality Matters, (https://www.qualitymatters.org) and Magna Teaching with Technology Conference (https://www.magnapubs.com).

Most disciplines have SoTL resources, even though they may not explicitly use the term SoTL. For example, the Council on Social Work Education (CSWE) publishes the *Journal of Social Work Education* and hosts an annual conference (https://www.cswe.org); likewise, the Association of Baccalaureate Social Work Program Directors (www.bpdonline.org) hosts a smaller conference. The American Psychological Association (www.apa.org) has a range of national and regional conferences and published journals for SoTL activities and research in psychology. Likewise, the American Association of Colleges of Nursing (http://www.aacnnursing.org/) hosts an annual conference and numerous webinars on higher education in nursing. Whether teaching accounting, zoology, or any combination, thereof, resources on effective teaching are available, and most of them have at least one journal and conference that is discipline specific. In addition, delving into disciplines distinct from your own is particularly fun and engaging. Interdisciplinary SoTL resources synthesize best practices across disciplines. These avenues provide opportunities for building your knowledge about teaching and learning and about contributing to SoTL.

In addition to these national and global opportunities, some universities or state and regional consortia provide SoTL resources. For example, we are members of the Kentucky Association of Social Work Educators and routinely present with colleagues and students at the annual conferences (e.g., Grise-Owens, et al., 2014; Grise-Owens, Miller, & White, 2007). Oftentimes, these local and regional presentations can be first steps in the development of more extensive scholarship by offering faculty (and students) an affordable and accessible forum to test SoTL ideas in a more informal setting. Likewise, university faculty development offices or a Faculty Development Committee on smaller campuses foster SoTL. We elaborate in Chapter 6 on avenues that foster learning communities to support ongoing engagement in SoTL.

We highly recommend for you to participate in these kinds of faculty development SoTL opportunities at a local, regional, national, or even international level. We urge you to dig into the SoTL literature early and often in your career. We echo Weimer's (2006) declaration about her own initial exposure to SoTL: "I felt as though it made me a better teacher almost immediately" (p. xi). SoTL is essential for a grounded and meaningful articulation of your philosophy. Perhaps even more so, SoTL is essential for sustaining your philosophy, practice, and spirit in this challenging and rewarding career.

We offer a caution regarding SoTL: Be cognizant of the expectations at your university. For example, the dominant culture of some Research I universities may not fully value the contributions and importance of SoTL. For instance, pragmatically, reviewers of promotion and tenure packets may dismiss or not even know about SoTL as a form or scholarship. In those contexts, you will need to interpret SoTL in ways that might not be necessary in other settings.

Keeping this caution in mind, we urge you not to allow these cultures to prevent you from engaging in SoTL and, indeed, promoting SoTL as a viable and significant form of scholarship. In Grise-Owens, Owens, & Miller, 2016a, we offer and discuss important recommendations for advancing SoTL in social work education, which apply to most disciplines and include the following: (a) Align more explicitly with the SoTL movement; (b) connect SoTL with accreditation processes; (c) reward SoTL work; (d) promote departmental, university, and discipline leadership that values SoTL; (e) expand ways of doing SoTL to include multiple formats and forums and student voices; (f) emphasize SoTL in doctoral programs; and (g) engage in critical, collegial conversations on how to use SoTL.

Elucidating Goodness of Fit and Sustaining the Mission

We have more than 40 years combined of teaching experience and have used a teaching–learning philosophy to inform, ground, and revitalize our practice for much of that time. Our initial articulation continues to deepen, as it is retested through our experiences in teaching and learning and participation in SoTL. In moving through the promotion and tenure process, we use our teaching–learning philosophy as an ongoing, central mechanism to describe our practice. In our promotion and tenure portfolios, as well as annual reviews, we further articulate and document the activation of our teaching–learning philosophy. As Goodyear and Allchin (1998) advised, we describe our teaching, service, and scholarship through the integrated lens of our philosophy. This synergistic strategy provides a consistent and engaging way to communicate our contributions, commitments, and competencies. Pragmatically, we believe it affects achieving promotion and tenure.

Similarly, articulation of your teaching philosophy should take into account how your teaching–learning approach fits with the university where you teach or hope to teach. *Goodness of fit*, a term used in research methods and in ecological theories, essentially refers to congruence or compatibility (Germain, 1991). For example, are your core values congruent with the mission of the university? Does the university mission statement and purpose converge with your philosophy statement and your core values and beliefs? Does the type of university (e.g., Research I university, liberal arts college, community and technical institution, private or public, and so forth) fit with your approach to teaching and your professional aspirations? In other words, does your personal mission (as explained in your philosophy) fit with the university, or perhaps on a smaller scale, the academic division or department? These are important questions to ask as you consider the congruency between your personal philosophy and the context.

Having an articulated teaching–learning philosophy has indelibly contributed to sustaining our passion for teaching. It has kept us grounded during some difficult times in our careers. We elaborate on the long-term impact of an activated philosophy in the final chapter of this book. However, we want to emphasize the importance of considering the long-term impact of your teaching philosophy even as you form your earliest iteration of it. Being intentional about examining the goodness of fit between your personal philosophy and the context in which you will be living that philosophy is important. For example, as noted earlier in the discussion about SoTL, you need to be aware of how the university culture views the faculty role of teaching, itself and, by extension, research on that teaching (i.e., SoTL).

This goodness of fit may change over the course of a career. For example, you may start out in a Research I institution and move to a teaching university, or the university where you teach may undergo significant changes with new leadership or take new directions. As we discuss in Chapter 6, these changes will likely influence a new iteration of your teaching philosophy. However, the initial process of articulation provides necessary clarity for grounding your philosophy and sustaining your philosophy through the changes over the course of a career.

As Weimer (2010) observed, "Most new college teachers start their careers full of enthusiasm for teaching [and then] teaching expectations collide with the realities of academic careers" (p. 149). She said that particularly when facing this collision, new faculty seek advice. She acknowledged the usefulness of advice, such as best practice strategies. However, she stated, "New faculty are better served with something other than advice. They need to acquire beliefs about teaching that position them for career-long growth and development" (p. 150).

Sustaining career-long growth and development requires an activated philosophy, and this activation begins with articulating your philosophy through reflecting on your values and beliefs as well as your experiences. Then, you use SoTL to inform and challenge those values, beliefs, and experiences. This process includes a consideration of goodness of fit among these facets. As we discuss in Chapter 6, reactivation involves continual iterations throughout your career. That is, your articulation is tested with implementation and evaluation, which clarifies and deepens your initial articulation.

Examples of Articulation

In this section we share briefly how we articulate our philosophy through reflecting on values, considering inductive experiences, engaging in SoTL, and assessing goodness of fit and sustaining mission. See Appendix B for brief examples of our teaching–learning philosophy statements, which are in an abbreviated form suitable for general information. As we state throughout the book, these brief statements become activated philosophies through deeper articulation, practical implementation, critical evaluation, and iterative reactivation. We illustrate throughout the book how we elaborate on our foundational philosophy statements in various forums, for example, promotion and tenure documents.

Additional samples of teaching statements can be found online. For example, many university faculty development offices put sample philosophies on their sites. See Appendix A for a list of a few illustrative sources. Professional education conferences often have workshops on developing a teaching philosophy statement. For example, Jogerst and Jackson (2017) provided a workshop presentation on writing a teaching philosophy statement at the Council on Social Work Education Annual Program Meeting.

Erlene's Articulation

I entered academia after several years of social work practice. Through reflection on the articulation questions posed throughout this chapter, and because I'm a word nerd, I determined my core values with alliteration using the first letter of my name, *E*. *Empowering* teaching and learning means everyone has equitable power, which includes accountability and responsibility. Deep, significant learning is meaning making, that is, *energizing*. Meaningful learning *engages* relationships between and among the teacher and learners, the lessons and real life. Deep learning *encompasses* contexts and roles beyond the classroom, such as a teaching–learning community in a broader world. Finally, teaching and learning is *evolving*. The educator and the student must consistently evaluate and adapt the processes and products of the shared teaching–learning community. These alliterative descriptors succinctly convey my core values in teaching and learning. Notably, I typically refer to my statement as a teaching and learning philosophy, which reflects my belief that unless learning is taking place, all teaching is moot: a core value. That is, I believe that if learning does not occur, then teaching is a fruitless exercise.

> I have used metaphors to further articulate my philosophy. For example, I wrote, I see the spiritual nature of my teaching as a quilt stitched from the myriad materials that come into my teaching–learning life, sometimes as rags of disappointment and dissonance and other times as fabric of discovery and delight. A Zen perspective provides the threads that hold together this patchwork perspective. (Grise-Owens, 2011, p. 150)

As noted earlier, a metaphor is an effective way to express a philosophy. This use of the metaphor encapsulated disparate aspects of my philosophy in a personal construct that is broadly accessible.

At first my teaching philosophy was largely inductive, based on my experiences and core values personally as well as professionally as a social worker. From my earliest memories, school was a favorite place to be. Also, my family placed a high value on education. I was drawn to a career in social work because of its commitment to service and social justice. I enjoyed clinical social work as I valued helping people reach their full potential; I enjoyed the administrator role in having organizational impact. Although I loved being a student, I had not considered being a full-time educator until I was invited by my alma mater to take a temporary faculty position. And I found my niche.

As a new educator, I drew from the many role models who had formed my love of learning and a few who had squelched it. I saw my role as educator as akin to my role as a therapist and administrator (i.e., promoting growth and change). I saw social work education as another arena of social work practice. That is, I believed the standards, values, and practices of my profession applied to the role of educator. These beliefs and experiences provided the initial formulation of my teaching philosophy even before I formally articulated it. For example, I knew that I learned best in an environment that engaged me as an active participant. I identified strongly with the social work core value of empowerment. As an administrator, I learned the importance of evaluation in evolving toward better outcomes.

I am chagrined to note that I did not know about SoTL until I had been teaching for several years. However, I was fortunate to obtain a doctorate in educational leadership. During my studies, I took several courses on theories of learning, philosophies of education, and teaching approaches. Certainly, an EdD is not necessary to have a grounded teaching philosophy. However, I do recommend reading foundational texts or taking doctoral courses on theories of learning and pedagogical and andragogical approaches (Driscoll, 2004).

Because I became intrigued with the feminist perspective and approaches to practice during my master's degree program, another early influence on my teaching–learning philosophy was feminist pedagogy. During my doctoral program, which coincided with the early formulation of my teaching philosophy, I immersed myself in the study of feminist pedagogy. In addition to materials from the American Association of University Women (http://www.aauw.org), I was radically affected by the iconic works of Belenky, Clinchy, Goldberger, and Tarule (1997); Goldberger, Tarule, Clinchy, and Belenky (1996); Maher and Tetreault (1994); and Minnich (1990). In the social work discipline, I was particularly informed by Figueira-McDonough, Netting, and Nichols-Casebolt (1998), who critiqued and challenged social work curricula. My dissertation, and some subsequent scholarship, was on sexism and social work education (Grise-Owens, 2002).

Feminist pedagogy principles include promoting empowerment, building community, ensuring all voices are heard, respecting diverse personal experiences, challenging traditional hegemonic views of theory and instruction, and reframing the roles and relationship of teacher and learner through power sharing (Brown, Collard, & Hoogeveen, 2014; Webb, Allen, & Walker, 2002). Notably, these feminist principles are reflected in my chosen profession of social work, which highlights social justice. Thus, these feminist and social work principles are distilled in the *Es* of my philosophy: *empowering, engaging, energizing, encompassing, and evolving.*

When I discovered SoTL, and the array of resources therein, my teaching–learning philosophy began to deepen exponentially. Fortunately, early social work educator mentors (especially my deans Diana Garland and Jillian Johnson) encouraged my participation at the Council on Social Work Education's annual conference. At this conference, I connected with other educators interested in enhancing our craft of teaching and of social work education in general. Then I began attending the Lilly Teaching Conference, the Teaching Professor Conference, and international conferences. I read works by authors such as those listed previously in the discussion on SoTL. These interdisciplinary experiences were pivotal in expanding my understanding of good teaching–learning practices and principles as well as connecting with others who simply loved teaching.

Notably these SoTL connections broadened my understanding of complementary pedagogy and andragogy, such as transformative, collaborative, and experiential approaches (Mezirow, 2000). Feminist pedagogy naturally expanded into criticalist and Freirian pedagogy and andragogy (hooks, 2003; Freire, 2007). Increasingly, I discovered a wealth of conceptual frameworks and pragmatic resources in educators such as Weimer (1993), Bain (2004), and Fink (2003). A book that synthesized these threads and crystallized my philosophy was written by a social work educator and five of her former students (Roche et al., 1999). I have read (and written) many SoTL products since my initial reading of this book, but it remains the most pivotal in solidifying my philosophy.

Quickly I began presenting and publishing in SoTL. This commitment to contributing to SoTL has the most impact on the activation of my philosophy. My teaching philosophy is expressed in Grise-Owens, 2011. Similar to Ada (2007), my activated teaching philosophy is a "search for a creative balance between idealism and practicality" (p. 105).

Reflecting on the trajectory of my career, I can readily see how the initial articulation of my teaching philosophy formed a solid and remarkably sustainable core. Although these five *Es* have certainly shall I say *evolved* (wink!), they have retained the essential values they originated from. My teaching philosophy has been the symbol and substance of my delight, devotion, and dedication in teaching. It has energized, deepened, challenged, and sustained my competence and contribution to a beloved profession. Without belaboring the vicissitudes of academia, I (like most long-term faculty) have experienced various challenges. Particularly in the challenging times, an activated philosophy provided a touchstone and compass keeping me grounded in my core values and providing direction for continued contribution and growth. I discuss this iterative process in Chapter 6.

As I noted earlier, my teaching philosophy is congruent with the core principles of my profession of social work, and in turn my choice of profession is congruent with my personal values. This congruence meant that my teaching philosophy fulfilled a professional mission and personal purpose.

Further, I taught for almost two decades at the same private university. Early I explicitly linked my philosophy with the university's mission statement by taking components of the university mission statement and connecting them with aspects of my teaching philosophy. For example, I linked *empowerment* with the university's mission component of *peace and social justice*, *engaging* with the component of *engaged community of learners*, and so forth. (See Appendix B for a full depiction of this linkage between my philosophy and the university mission.) Certainly, this linkage underscored the goodness of fit between my personal philosophy and the university's mission. Pragmatically, I elaborated on these linkages in promotion and tenure documents, annual reviews, and other processes. This close linkage between my individual philosophy and the university's mission was a framework for providing compelling evidence of contribution and congruence. Ultimately, the erosion of this linkage as the university's leadership became less congruent with the stated mission became emblematic of my severance from the university. See Chapter 6 for the rest of that story!

Larry's Articulation

I entered academia full-time after 25 years in the nonprofit sector as a child welfare administrator. In articulating my teaching philosophy, I reflected on my years of experience in social work practice before making the transition to an academic role. I even use the term *pracademic* to refer to those who blend the role of practitioner and academic (Owens, 2016). I view the role of education as primarily to prepare graduates for the profession and prepare them to function as world citizens. I agree with Brookfield's (1995) assertion that what happens in educational settings "changes the world" (p. 266).

Thus, my teaching philosophy facets include an integrative framework and relevant application; supportive mentoring; communication emphasis; and an interactive approach. These facets have the overarching goal of making course content applicable to the social work practice settings in a diverse, global context. As an administrator I hired and supervised hundreds of people in a social work setting. I understand the knowledge, skills, and values needed to be successful in the profession. Further, I see myself as a global citizen and see the need for the profession of social work to take an international perspective. Thus, I bring that background to my role in the academic setting in preparing students to thrive in the helping profession. My philosophy emphasizes supporting students in their professional development, incorporates my core values and beliefs, and emphasizes the unique talents and experiences I bring to the learning process as a pracademic and global citizen.

Likewise, I'm able to take my own inductive experience in the social work practice setting and my educational preparation to inform and shape my philosophy. I worked with a multitude of new professionals in my work as an administrator. My philosophy emphasizes one of the roles I enjoyed and found essential: supportive mentoring. A number of the staff I worked with commented that my support and encouragement played a significant role in completing their academic degrees. Although staff members who obtained their degree often meant they would leave the organization for a different position, I relished the opportunity to support them in the same manner that I was encouraged in my professional development. This mentoring role and encouraging staff development readily translates to my faculty role (Jensen, 2017).

In addition, as an introvert and hands-on learner, my own educational experience influenced my philosophy of using an interactive approach and relevant application in the classroom. In my earliest memories of school, I struggled with the traditional learning environments. I recognize from my experience and reading the literature that different learning styles (Kolb, 1984) along with multiple intelligences and ways of understanding (Gardner, 2011) have an impact on learning. I seek to create a classroom and learning environment that helps student thrive and learn. I use multiple learning techniques and strategies to stimulate critical thinking, promote learning, and encourage the application of knowledge to the social work practice setting.

Similar to Erlene's experience, my EdD in educational leadership curriculum helped ground me in teaching–learning theories and practices. Likewise, my experience and investment in developing leadership skills in my practice readily transferred to the faculty role. In effect, I view the faculty role as a leadership function. A favorite leadership resource, Collins (2001) asserts that great leaders should focus on "first who, then what" (p. 41). I view my faculty role as the first who of developing capable social workers for social work practice. Not only do I see my faculty role as a leadership function but I see it as developing future social work leaders. Brilliant (1986) spoke of the lack of emphasis on leadership preparation as the missing link in the social work profession. She noted that "leadership has no prominence in the social work curriculum" (p. 327). Although Brilliant made this assertion more than 30 years ago, little has changed (Owens, Call, & Vincent, 2017). I see one of my primary roles as developing social workers for practice, which includes the development of leaders for our social work organizations.

In a related application, throughout my experiences in social work management positions, my approach to leadership has been similar to Lao Tzu's (1989) assertion that great leaders are ones whose presence is barely noticed. He further says that with this style of leadership, after a great task is completed, people don't look to the leader but instead look to each other and declare, "We ourselves have achieved it!" (p. 35). Likewise, in my teaching, a measure of success is when students exclaim, "Look what we achieved." The policy course adaptation described in Chapter 4 illustrates this point. Students' experiences moved from completing an assignment for the professor to assess to Look what we did.

The introduction to and involvement in SoTL has been invaluable in my development as an educator. Fortunately, I was connected with others in social work education who had been immersed in SoTL for many years; they helped me get a jump-start in this arena. Quickly, I was introduced to the literature on SoTL. As an adjunct faculty, I had been attending the CSWE annual conferences and soon began presenting. I've presented at numerous SoTL conferences, such as the International Lilly Conference on College Teaching, the Teaching Professor Conference, and the Wakonse Conference on College Teaching.

In my first year at my current university, I was assigned a faculty mentor in a different department. In our first meeting, he said, "You don't have to get tenure alone." He advised working with multiple partners and colleagues and to always be working on several projects at once. This stellar advice prompted me to be part of several writing groups on a range of research topics. Now that I have tenure, I'm paying it forward and meeting one of the tenets of my philosophy. I am intentional about being a supportive mentor to junior faculty and involving them in research projects, which include the SoTL areas of understanding the faculty experience at branch campuses, identifying faculty perceptions of academic leaders, and understanding social work education as an arena of social work practice.

Similarly, my success as a social work educator has been greatly enhanced by the goodness of fit between my teaching philosophy and the university where I teach. My interests in global issues and the infusion of international content into my courses fits with my university's vision to be "a leading American university with international reach." (Western Kentucky University, n.d.). With emphases on teaching and preparation for the profession, the university and department recognize my value as a pracademic. My teaching philosophy accentuates an integrative framework, relevant application, and communication emphasis in the academic unit. These principles of my philosophy and my extensive social work practice experience enable me to better prepare students for their own future as professional social workers. Further, there is a goodness of fit between my pracademic status and philosophy emphases and being the social work faculty site leader at one of our university's branch campuses.

Furthermore, my philosophy achieves further goodness of fit by linking it to professional competencies (see Appendix C). Similar to how social work education programs must link their curriculum to professional competencies, I have clearly linked my teaching philosophy to those same competencies and the broader interprofessional competencies. In so doing, I demonstrate how my philosophy of teaching meets the expectations of our profession. By extension, these linkages support my university and department in their accreditation efforts to show "how its faculty models the behaviors and values of the profession in the program's educational environment" (CSWE, 2015, p. 16).

Finally, I want to discuss briefly how my teaching philosophy mirrors the values of my profession of social work. Specifically, social work emphasizes social justice. This emphasis encompasses equity, fairness, and human rights, which includes attention to power, privilege, and oppression. As a cisgender straight White male who is in a professional role, I must be cognizant of the privilege inherent in these identities. My teaching approach involves acknowledging this privilege and modeling the use of this privilege to challenge inequitable systems including the hegemonic approaches to education.

Jay's Articulation

Like Larry and Erlene, I entered the academy after several years of social work practice. Indubitably, these professional experiences have shaped the way I view teaching and learning and subsequently how I articulate my philosophy.

The articulation of one's philosophy is profoundly affected by identity. Palmer (1998) asserted that "good teaching cannot be reduced to technique; good teaching comes from the identity and integrity of the teacher" (p. 10). Your identity will inherently shape your experience, which in turn will shape your teaching and learning (Dewey, 1938; Freire, 2007a, b).

Like most people, my identity is complex. I am a millennial. I am a person of color. I am male in a profession that is overwhelmingly female. I spent time in out-of-home care as a young person and went on to practice social work in a variety of contexts at local, state, and federal levels. I am fervently dedicated to service. These and other experiences have had an impact on the conceptualization and articulation of my philosophy.

In terms of my journey in the academy, my career as an educator began at a small teaching school. I was fortunate to connect with a mentor who loved teaching and was already invested in SoTL. During these formative years, I engaged in SoTL in a way that I am not sure I would've been able to in another environment. I began to conduct classroom research with colleagues and really assess and test approaches to teaching and learning. My interactions with students and colleagues, viewed through my own positionality, crystalized my thoughts about education. Concomitantly, these thoughts were influenced through interaction with SoTL.

My philosophy is rooted in constructivist and criticalist perspectives. That is, one of my values is to recognize that everyone in the learning community has knowledge to contribute. Against this backdrop, I articulate a liberatory approach to teaching and learning. Liberatory is a process defined as, "tending to set free. … To be liberatory is to construct, in concert with others, the conditions and to engage in the critical inquiry and connective dialogue that makes liberation more likely" (Roche et al., 1999, xiii). This description of liberatory serves as the foundation for my teaching–learning philosophy.

Akin to Erlene's experience, my approach was inspired by Roche et al. (1999), which was written by faculty and students. I read this book as a graduate student and since then have read it countless times. This text encouraged me to more critically explore transformative, active, and experiential learning theories and to examine the works of Dewey (1938), Freire (2007 a.b), Kolb (1984), and Mezirow (1990), among others.

My philosophy emphasizes co-constructed knowledge (e.g., teacher-learner partnerships) and views the classroom as a microcosm of the broader world (Birkenmaier et al., 2011; Fox, 2013; Goldstein, 2001; Grise-Owens, Miller, & Owens, 2016; hooks, 2003; Saleebey & Scanlon, 2005). Simply put, one's way of knowing is simply *a* way and not *the* way.

My approach encapsulates a holistic experience of the education process and revolves around a central premise: The classroom is a community of participants. Barker (2003) defined a community as a group of individuals who share and have investment in a distinct value set. Bain (2004) asserted that optimal teaching operates on a similar premise that everyone works in unison toward a common goal. Developing a nourishing sense of community is perhaps the most important aspect of teaching (McKeachie & Svinicki, 2006). Classroom environments offer the best potential for learning when they operate as a healthy, united community.

Around this central premise of community, my philosophy is rooted in three core principles: co-constructed knowledge, revisioned (redefined) educational spaces, and human rights and social change. Again, these guiding principles are influenced by my personal and professional experiences, and these elements of my philosophy are congruent with the values of my professional discipline, such as service, social justice, dignity and worth of individuals, and the importance and centrality of human relationships (National Association of Social Workers [NASW], 2017). Further, they are consistent with the mission and values of the land-grant public institution where I teach now. Ultimately, these connections help with the goodness of fit.

Later in the book we all share our thoughts about how actualizing the teaching philosophy helps to sustain us in academe. However, I want to make one point clear, which I reiterate in Chapter 6. We all view the teaching philosophy as a living thing, meaning that as you evolve as an individual, your teaching will also likely evolve. As you continue to learn about teaching and learning and engage in the implementation and evaluation of your philosophy, you will glean insights on elements of your philosophy you want to carry forward, and some you don't.

For me, my most profound insight into articulating my philosophy is realizing that "MY philosophy is not all about ME" (Owens et al., 2014, p. 340). To the contrary, articulating my philosophy is about the broader learning community in which I operate. In this way, the articulation of my philosophy becomes a vehicle for my own learning about learning. I trust that as I continue to learn and to change so too will my philosophy. ■

Chapter 4

Now That I Have One, How Do I Implement My Teaching Philosophy?

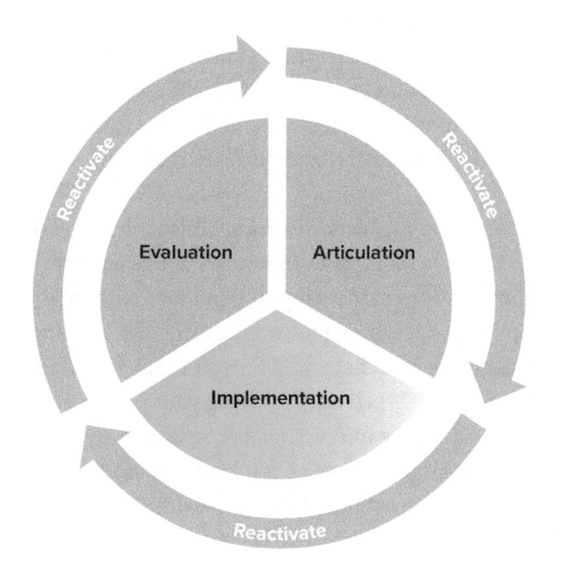

This chapter describes the implementation phase, how it relates to articulation and evaluation, and the value of this phase. Using examples from our own teaching experiences to illustrate, we show you how to pragmatically link an articulated philosophy with concrete practice. Emphatically, these examples are illustrative, not exhaustive nor prescriptive. We want to give you some specific ideas on how to implement a teaching philosophy. But, just as the articulation of your philosophy must be individualized, the implementation must fit your philosophy, specific courses, curricular parameters, and so forth. These examples will give you some ideas of how to get started in implementing your activated philosophy.

Similar to the articulation section in Chapter 3, this section uses the following guiding questions to help you design the implementation of your teaching philosophy: What in your actual teaching demonstrates or tests your articulated philosophy? What class assignments, classroom activities, learning environment expectations and norms implement your teaching philosophy? Is there congruence between what you say you do and teach and what students are learning? How do you address power, privilege, and diversity? How do your assessment methods reflect your teaching philosophy?

Practically, this phase involves moving beyond articulating a teaching philosophy to putting the philosophy into praxis. Key elements in this phase include (a) sharing the teaching philosophy with colleagues and students (b) designing and developing a classroom culture and learning environment that are congruent with the teaching philosophy, (c) identifying specific assignments and activities that demonstrate the teaching philosophy, and (d) selecting modes of assessment congruent with the teaching philosophy.

Sharing Your Teaching Philosophy

An initial element in implementing a teaching philosophy is sharing the philosophy with learners and colleagues. Akin to our belief that all social work practitioners should discuss their modalities with clients and colleagues (DuBois & Miley, 2011), likewise, we believe all educators should share their philosophy of teaching with learners and other faculty members (Goodyear & Allchin, 1998). Prior to the beginning of a new course, we make our teaching philosophy accessible to the class or learning community. We state that this transparency about our approach vis-à-vis our philosophy is modeling how our students should practice with their constituents and clients. We post a copy of our teaching philosophy using the learning management system software (Blackboard, Moodle) and discuss it in the first class meeting. As O'Brien, Millis, and Cohen (2008) asserted, sharing your philosophy with students "clarifies what you value about the instructional process and lays a foundation that justifies why you've organized the course as you have" (p. 45).

Additionally, we share our teaching philosophy with faculty colleagues by making it part of professional development and evaluation documents as well as collegial discussions. As noted earlier, an activated teaching philosophy can be shared through digital formats. Faculty can use programs such as Glogster, WeExplore, and other interactive multimedia platforms to create, update, and share the ongoing activation of teaching philosophies. As we suggest in Chapter 6, ideally academic units should have a shared teaching–learning philosophy or at least a shared understanding of the faculty members' teaching philosophies. Finally, we share aspects of our teaching philosophy in the public sphere through SoTL contributions. Throughout this book, we emphasize the important connection between an activated teaching philosophy and SoTL.

Sharing a teaching philosophy actualizes your approach in observable ways. This actualization fulfills two distinct yet interconnected purposes in the implementation, namely, credibility and accountability. Thus, in implementation the philosophy moves beyond an articulated ideal to become visible and viable.

First, being explicit and open about your teaching philosophy provides you with credibility among learners and faculty colleagues. Realistically, students often perform classroom tasks and assignments at the behest of the instructor without knowing or considering why they are performing these activities (Naidoo & Jamieson, 2005; Potts, 2005). Being transparent about the foundation of our teaching philosophy and the impact this philosophy has had on the development of the course helps students understand the purpose of the course, learning tasks, and the rationale for approaching these tasks in particular ways. This credibility is foundational for the effective implementation of the teaching philosophy and leads to a more effective completion of assignments by students (O'Brien, Millis, & Cohen, 2008).

Notably, we do not belabor the philosophy in the first meeting; rather, we introduce it to convey an initial understanding of our approach. Then, as we illustrate in our discussion later, we demonstrate the philosophy through the ongoing structure, teaching–learning style, selection of assignments, and assessment modes. We agree with Fox's (2011, 2013) assertion that faculty should model, mirror, and mentor. Building on his excellent work, we propose that the implementation of the teaching philosophy should model best practices, mirror professional values, and mentor students toward competency.

Pragmatically, this modeling, mirroring, and mentoring is accomplished through several functions in the implementation phase of activating a teaching philosophy. First, we give the rationale for assignments as linked with our teaching philosophy, the values of the profession, and the professional competencies promoted through the assignment. Likewise, we consistently clarify how these linkages play out in the structure and culture of our classes, and we explain how evaluative measures are congruent with our teaching philosophy. If there is incongruence, we acknowledge that and explain why that is so. For example, sometimes university policies might require us to treat students in a fashion that is not congruent with our teaching philosophy. At times we brainstorm with students about ways to moderate those policies in a manner that is more in accordance with our teaching philosophy. This discussion about congruence begins in the introduction of the teaching philosophy and is sustained throughout the course and indeed across courses.

Similar to making your teaching philosophy transparent with students, sharing your teaching philosophy with colleagues builds credibility. This sharing can occur through collegial communications and formal documents, such as promotion and tenure processes and through informal collegial conversations. These conversations may be more formally structured through faculty development opportunities. For example, we have initiated or participated in faculty book clubs or discussion groups that explicitly engaged participants in conversation about aspects of our activated teaching philosophy. Transparency about how you implement your teaching philosophy and your ongoing attention to its activation gives credence to your investment in teaching and provides substantive evidence of a grounded approach to your professional role of teaching.

Second, in a complementary fashion, sharing your teaching philosophy serves as an accountability mechanism. The teaching philosophy sets parameters for all those in the learning community. From the student's perspective, being transparent about the teaching philosophy assists students in understanding the expectations of the course. In turn, students can hold the faculty member accountable for fulfilling the expectations expressed in the teaching philosophy. This accountability also encourages attention to power dynamics and diversity considerations. For example, our teaching philosophies articulate the importance of discussion and dialogue in the learning process. Hence, students are empowered (and encouraged) to let us know if we use too many lectures, do not permit adequate time for discussion, or if certain voices are being marginalized.

Similarly, when colleagues are aware of our philosophy, they are able to offer critical and constructive feedback about assignments or activities not congruent with our philosophy. Likewise, sharing teaching philosophies encourages collegial dialogue about ways to promote effective teaching and learning and strengthen curricula. Ideally, this increased accountability allows more cohesive learning experiences for the learning community across the curriculum for students and faculty.

Finally, engaging in SoTL is a way of sharing one's teaching philosophy with a broad audience of peers, or the teaching commons. As we clarified in Chapter 3, SoTL is purposeful, reflective, documented, and shared in public evaluative forums, which contributes to the knowledge base (Shulman, 2000; Wang, 2012; Weimer, 2010). In essence, SoTL is active learning about teaching that is shared with others with the intent of enriching teaching and learning (Grise-Owens, Owens, & Miller, 2016a).

This SoTL engagement promotes credibility and accountability for the faculty member in a professional context. By contributing to SoTL, you make public your teaching philosophy, whether parts of it or as a whole. Next, we describe approaches, assignments, and assessments that show the implementation of our philosophies. We demonstrate that most of these examples are documented through our SoTL contributions. This synergistic approach to teaching and scholarship mutually informs and strengthens teaching and scholarship (Albers, 2003; Bishop-Clark & Dietz-Uhler, 2012; McKinney, 2007, 2013; Weimer, 2006) and promotes accountability and credibility.

SoTL is an important thread throughout an activated philosophy. As we discussed earlier, SoTL is an important venue for learning about theories and approaches that can inform your philosophy. Chapter 5 explains how SoTL serves as an important evaluative process. SoTl informs and refines all phases of an activated philosophy.

Designing and Developing a Congruent Classroom Culture

As the teaching philosophy is made public, you must ensure all aspects of the course are designed in accordance with the philosophy. The overall culture of the class, including course objectives, guidelines, and selection of course materials, should be rooted in and indicative of the philosophy. Every aspect of the syllabus should reflect your philosophy. Likewise, every aspect of your philosophy should be evident in your syllabus, and we do mean every aspect, from the presentation of ways to contact you to the policies about absences, grading, and so forth, and to the actual assignments. Weimer (2010) pointed out that every aspect of our teaching is based on assumptions. So you must consistently ask yourself if the values and beliefs you espouse in your teaching philosophy are present or are unrecognized assumptions at play. Here again, attention to the dynamics of power, privilege, diversity, and marginalization must be explicitly considered.

The syllabus has a significant impact on the socialization to the course and indelibly affects the entire learning process (Albers, 2003; Caughlin, 2014; Cullen, 2013; Harrington & Gabert-Quillen, 2015; Jenkins, Bugeja, & Barber, 2014; Lang, 2016; Saville, Zinn, Brown, & Marchuk, 2010). Many online resources are available to aid with constructing syllabi, usually through university centers for teaching and learning. O'Brien, Millis, and Cohen (2008) provide a comprehensive workbook for designing a syllabus, which includes excellent resource lists ranging from online sources to readings on course and curriculum design. Dedicating time to learning about syllabus design is particularly applicable for an activated teaching philosophy. Pragmatically, your syllabus should be a blueprint of your teaching philosophy.

In addition to the more detailed teaching statement we make available to students, we include a one-paragraph summary of our teaching philosophy on all syllabi (Mandernach, 2009). The following is an example from a syllabus for a course that Jay and Erlene team taught, which melded their complementary philosophies:

> As co-faculty, we share a liberatory, criticalist approach to teaching–learning. Liberatory is a process defined as, "tending to set free . . . To be liberatory is to construct, in concert with others, the conditions and to engage in the critical inquiry and connective dialogue that makes liberation more likely." (From Roche et al., 1999, xiii, in *Contesting the Boundaries in Social Work Education: A Liberatory Approach*). We believe teaching–learning should be empowering, engaging, energizing, encompassing, and evolving. We will elaborate on this approach in the first class and invite you to join us in developing a healthy and sustainable teaching–learning community.

As noted earlier, the first class of all our courses includes a presentation and explicit discussion on the teaching philosophy and how this philosophy affects the course. This discussion allows critical dialogue related to the approach and sets the tone for the class environment.

After the introduction of the teaching philosophy and student introductions, we lead the class or learning community in establishing group guidelines that explain how we operate and move forward with learning experiences. These group guidelines are posted on the learning management system software and are revisited throughout the course as needed. In some instances, these group guidelines follow a cohort of students throughout a sequence of courses with adaptations made in each new course. This approach builds a teaching–learning community that is owned by the students (Dean, 2007; Lang, 2016; Pyles & Adam, 2016). For us, developing these guidelines in the context of discussing the teaching philosophy ensures a classroom culture consistent with the central premises of our philosophies, for example, an empowering, engaging, interactive approach.

Then we review the syllabus and expectations for the course. Even the way we conduct this review reflects our teaching philosophies. For instance, all our teaching philosophies include an element of student engagement and empowerment. So we usually provide opportunities for students to negotiate details of the course structure. These negotiations may include due dates, selection of assignments, details of an activity, and so forth. This power sharing should ensure that faculty are providing the structure and expertise necessary for promoting student confidence and maintaining efficiency while ensuring shared student input and a meaningful impact on the learning processes and environment (Weimer, 2002, 2013; Vella, 2002).

Here is an example of that balance. In a graduate-level course on social work practice with groups, the syllabus assigned group presentations on various aspects of group dynamics. When Erlene began teaching the course, the syllabus listed assigned topics. To foster student engagement and model best practices, she revised the assignment. In the first class, she led the class in an exercise in which they identified (a) what we know about group dynamics and (b) what we want to learn about group dynamics. This discussion allowed students to claim their knowledge and have an investment in the chosen targets for advancing their knowledge. Then students self-selected into groups based on the topic they were most interested in. Typically, topics included core group facilitation skills, dealing with conflict in groups, and so forth. As anticipated, students typically selected the same topics the instructor previously had assigned; however, the investment in the assignment was notably more evident in the caliber of their presentations.

Enactment of your teaching philosophy should also be intentional in relation to the teaching learning community's culture or climate. We strive to increase a sense of connection and community, whether in face-to-face or online environments because it deepens student knowledge (Lang, 2016). For online courses, we strive for social presence through consistent, open communications and building group cohesion (Bowen, 2012; Caulfield, 2011; Richardson, & Swan, 2003; Weisenberg, & Stacey, 2005). The examples given here are used in face-to-face, hybrid, or online environments.

The first class sets the tone for the course and is a key test of congruence between your stated philosophy and its implementation (Lang, 2016; Peters &

Weisberg, 2011). For example, because our teaching philosophies embrace student empowerment, engagement, and co-constructed knowledge, we design the first class to include meaningful introductions and connections between co-learners and teachers and the course content and goals. Introductions matter, and many creative and useful strategies can be used (Caulfield, 2011; Weimer, 2013).

For example, in introducing ourselves we tell them why we enjoy teaching that particular course and explain its relevance. Likewise, we ask students to share their experiences and feelings about the course, negative and positive. In another example, across a semester students share their selected theme song with the class. In each class one or two students tell the group what their selection is and why it is their theme song. We introduce ourselves on the first day by also sharing our theme song in that manner. By the end of the course, we have a distinctive class CD that makes a memorable connection. Simple exercises, such as these, can have a powerful effect on building community.

Congruence between the teaching philosophy and the learning community culture is inextricably linked with the concept of implicit curriculum (IC), also called the hidden curriculum. The impact of IC is increasingly recognized. For example, the CSWE (2015) standards require social work programs to give significant attention to the implicit curriculum, which emphasizes the impact of the learning environment or culture. Likewise, other disciplines, particularly medicine and education, are attentive to the importance of IC (Agrawal, Szatmari, & Hanson, 2008; Balmer, Master, Richards, & Giardino, 2009; Billings, Engelbert, Curtis, Block, & Sullivan, 2010; Eisner, 2002; Gofton, & Regehr, 2006).

The CSWE (2015) defined IC as the "learning environment in which the explicit curriculum is presented, [and] it is as important as the Explicit Curriculum in shaping students' professional character and competence" (p. 14). IC is communicated through philosophy, policies, procedures, and processes; it radiates through every aspect of the teaching–learning context and is a "critical set of variables influencing what students learn" (Holloway et al. 2008, p. 3). Attention to IC is particularly important for responsible attention to diversity. Students and faculty come from myriad cultural backgrounds; we all bring diverse social identities and intersectional positionalities that affect how the student and faculty view and interpret every aspect of the educational experience. Everything from the student handbook to faculty feedback to classroom norms is viewed through diverse lenses.

A growing body of literature documents adverse experiences of students in the educational experience related to marginalized social identities (Blankenship & Stewart, 2017; Boysen, 2012; Moore, 2016; Ohito, 2016; Steele, Spencer, & Aronson, 2002; Winans-Solis, 2014). From silencing female voices to privileging White Eurocentric culture to heteronormative bias to microaggressions, microinequities, and stereotype threat, these dynamics play out in every aspect of education. As we discuss later, these adverse student experiences are often mirrored in the experiences of faculty from marginalized groups. Thus, faculty must know how to ameliorate marginalization and disempowerment as part of their teaching roles. Concomitantly, effective educational environments must intentionally access and honor diversity. Activated teaching philosophies consider these important aspects.

Clearly for the development of competent graduates, congruence between the explicit curriculum (content) and the implicit curriculum (culture) is particularly key (Balmer et al., 2009; Bogo & Wayne, 2013; Christiansen, 2016; Grise-Owens, Eaves, & Miller, 2013; Miller, 2013; Peterson et al., 2014). Using an activated teaching philosophy is perhaps the most effective way to ensure congruence between the explicit curriculum and implicit curriculum. Individually and programmatically, faculty must continuously reflect on the congruence between their teaching philosophy and approaches (how and what they teach) and what they are expecting students to learn. For example, if students are expected to learn how to be competent in professionalism, their courses should promote a culture conducive to demonstrating those skills and have assignments that build those skills. The teaching philosophy is the framework for defining and developing this congruence.

Identifying Assignments and Activities

Another essential element of implementing a teaching philosophy is developing class tasks, exercises, and assignments congruent with the teaching philosophy, which involves the details of what you actually do to enact your stated philosophy. Although our teaching philosophies vary in some ways, our philosophies consistently emphasize similar values, such as an empowered and engaged learning environment, as well as the congruence between assignments and practice realities. Next we provide several examples of how we implement our teaching philosophies.

As an overarching way of implementing our teaching philosophy, we and other colleagues have used a specific ongoing assignment titled Indicators of Professionalism (IOP) in many of our courses (Grise-Owens & Jones, 2014; Grise-Owens & Steen, 2013). Many of the problematic behaviors that cause faculty frustration and hinder student success, such as arriving on time, being prepared, interacting collegially, and so forth, are indicators of professionalim. Developing professionalism is an explicit aim in professional disciplines (Keaton, 2015; Miller, 2013).

In our syllabi, this IOP assignment is introduced as follows:

> This course promotes a professional learning community model. This structure assumes the active participation of mature learners who take responsibility for their own learning and are committed to a collaborative work style. Learners are expected to demonstrate professional behaviors appropriate to an employment role and setting. The professional behavior will be assessed for course credit, using the following criteria: Preparation, Presence, and Participation.

Each of these criteria are explained. For example, the presence criterion includes an attendance policy. The assessment rubric of these criteria is adapted to fit the class structure, whether online, hybrid, or face-to-face formats; number of class meetings or other participation modes; and so forth.

Routinely, throughout the course, students self-assess on these criteria (using points allotted to the assignment). The professor gives feedback on the self-report rubric, and if the student and professor disagree, they discuss this discrepancy. This collegial approach promotes self-monitoring and consistent oversight. For example, a student may be too lenient and not deduct the required points for lateness (as designated on the syllabus); other times, a student may be too harsh and deduct too many points. Both examples are opportunities for the faculty member to engage the student in a dialogue about professionalism and on diverse cultural norms about such concepts as lateness, professional dress, and so forth. This dialogue helps students learn to navigate the possible dissonance among personal, cultural, and dominant professional norms.

Notably, students routinely report that this assignment promotes a high level of accountability and professional growth. The IOP promotes competencies in professional comportment, ethical accountability, critical reflection, and evaluation. The IOP and similar assignments promote a classroom culture that mirrors professional competencies and is congruent with our teaching philosophies, which emphasize relevant application, empowerment, and mutual responsibility and accountability.

In another example, when we discuss a reading in class, we emphasize that every participant (student, faculty, and author) has power in constructing the meaning of that reading. Every person brings different life experiences, positionalities, and so forth to the reading. In the broader world, some knowing is privileged above others, and left unchallenged, the classroom can mimic that power dynamic. However, justice requires challenging that hegemony through co-constructing knowledge (Adams, Bell, & Griffin, 2007; Baker, Jensen, & Kolb, 2002; Birkenmaier et al., 2011; Van Soest & Garcia, 2003). This shared power approach implements our philosophies.

Here we offer an example of how attention to implementation of a teaching philosophy affected an undergraduate social welfare policy course that Larry teaches. Traditionally the major assignment in the course was writing a paper on a social policy concern. This assignment was not congruent with Larry's teaching philosophy, and as a result did not have satisfactory learning outcomes. Larry redesigned the course in the following manner. Students were placed in groups of four to five. Each group selected a social welfare problem or issue with policy implications at the state level. Each group completed a detailed analysis of a problem or issue and identified current or proposed legislation that addressed their problem or issue. Based on their analysis, each group proposed a change to the policy or the legislation on their problem or issue. This proposed policy change was written in the format of a bill or legislative or administrative regulation. Finally, a state legislator and a social welfare lobbyist were invited to the class, and each group presented its proposed policy change to the legislator and lobbyist who provided feedback and a critique of their proposed policy change.

This change in the policy course assignment met the tenets of Larry's teaching philosophy of relevant application, communication emphasis, and interactive approach. Students learned the skill of writing legislation in bill format and presenting their idea to an actual policy maker. Further, students were able to see the legislator as a real person who was approachable and receptive to their ideas on improving the social welfare system. Finally, the change in the course assignment introduced the students to state legislation and regulations in a manner that students found meaningful and accessible. This redesign of the course resulted in improved student engagement and learning outcomes, including understanding their professional role and responsibility in affecting social policies. The redesign was precipitated by reflection on the incongruence between the espoused teaching philosophy and design of the course. This example illustrates how a faculty member should consistently assess the relationship between the articulated philosophy and actual course assignments.

The following is an example of the congruent implementation of a teaching philosophy in a social work practice course sequence that Erlene and Jay team taught. Our teaching philosophy views social action assignments as empowering and active learning experiences for students to build practice competency through relevant application. As such, we developed a social action meta project (Grise-Owens, Miller, & Owens, 2014). This assignment, which we implemented in a graduate-level advanced generalist practice course sequence, required students to research a global social justice issue, educate the community about that issue, and participate in an activism initiative aimed at addressing the issue. This assignment encouraged students to venture beyond the confines of the traditional classroom to explore global connections that span social work practice contexts.

Another example of an assignment consistent with a teaching philosophy occurs in Jay's undergraduate research class. This assignment requires students to begin to think about and conceptualize their own research agenda. Aspects of this assignment require students to select an area of social work and populations they are interested in knowing more about, develop research questions, and delineate explicit strategies and sources for gathering literature pertaining to their expressed interest area. Subsequent class exercises and assignments are based explicitly on this agenda. This work allows students to grapple with concepts such as sampling, research design, data collection, and statistical analysis in a context that not only interests them but is one they created. This assignment is conducive with Jay's teaching philosophy to empower students to take ownership not only of what they learn but how they learn it. This investment promotes a systematic understanding of research concepts and fosters an increased synergy in the teaching–learning community.

As we mentioned earlier, philosophies should be specific enough to be meaningful over time; concomitantly, they should be general enough to be adaptable as educational information and contexts change. Here we present an overall example of this adaptation. Particularly with the growing use of technology in teaching and learning, the flipped classroom is increasingly understood as key for effective learning (Bowen, 2012; Lage, Platt, & Treglia, 2000; Sage & Sele, 2015). In short, this approach describes class structures that move information modes (such as extensive lectures) to outside class time; the in-class time focuses on students doing things such as engaging in critical discussions, problem solving, application exercises, group presentations, and so forth (Lang, 2017). The examples given here amply illustrate how our teaching philosophies are adaptable to this changing structure. For instance, our philosophy tenets of engaging, relevant application, and co-constructed knowledge are congruent with the flipped classroom structure (Jensen, Kummer, & Godoy, 2015). Indeed, because our philosophies are grounded in solid educational principles, such as active learning, we had been using the flipped classroom structure before the term came into vogue. Now, in continued activation of our philosophies, we contribute to the SoTL literature about this approach and benefit from the expanding knowledge base about it.

We have provided an array of examples of how our teaching philosophies are implemented through actual course assignments and even curricular emphases. Also, we demonstrated how to integrate SoTL as a means of activating your teaching philosophy. These examples are illustrative, but you must design assignments and activities that are congruent with your philosophy and, if not congruent, evaluate how they should be changed. Ultimately, activation of your philosophy requires being attentive to the congruence in every aspect of your courses. We recommend intentional and ongoing review of your syllabi and class agendas as a concrete way of monitoring this congruence.

Selecting Modes of Assessment

In addition to the congruence between your philosophy and course assignments and activities, a philosophy manifests itself in the way you assess assignments (O'Brien, Millis, & Cohen, 2008; Walvoord & Andersen, 2010). Although framed for assessment at a university level, the principles of the American Association of Higher Education (1991) play out in individual classrooms and through individual philosophies. These principles state that effective assessment (a) begins with educational values; (b) views learning as multidimensional, integrated, and occurs over time; (c) works best with clear, explicitly stated purposes; (d) requires attention to both outcomes and experiences; (e) is ongoing, not episodic; (f) fosters wide involvement; (g) illuminates what people care about and use; (h) is part of a larger set of conditions that foster change; and (i) meets responsibilities to students and to the public.

As stated earlier, our teaching philosophies value ideals such as interactive engagement, co-constructed knowledge, and relevant application. Thus, evaluation modes mirror these ideals. Consequently, the overall grades for many assignments are calculations of instructor, peer, and self-evaluation scores. We emphasize how the use of multimodal assessment mirrors the practice world and the profession's values; this framing reinforces our teaching philosophy and promotes learner investment. For example, students typically resist self and peer evaluations (Anastas, 2010). However, we clarify that as professional practitioners they will need to have the skills to self-assess and provide collegial feedback. This framing in the context of our teaching philosophy reinforces the relevance of these assessment modes.

Particularly when assigning group work, the evaluative methods incorporate collegial feedback. Also, congruent with our teaching philosophy, we incorporate self-assessments routinely. Using self and peer assessments encourages engagement and deepens learning (Angelo & Cross, 1993; Walvoord & Anderson, 2010). Notably, we often include instructor assessment of the caliber of the peer or self-review. This assessment might be more informal or a graded assignment. This approach serves to promote internalized accountability and professional growth (Weimer, 2002; Miller, Grise-Owens, Drury, & Rickman, 2017).

For example, we use professional development plans (PDPs) as assignments. Students self-assess their competence in a specific area (e.g., writing, presenting, self-care), identifying strengths and areas for improvement. Then they determine specific strategies for growth. They use their PDPs as a self-monitoring tool, which may be revised over time during a particular course or throughout their progression in the program. We grade the assignment on the caliber of their self-critique. Typically, we use the following: Is their assessment and plan clear, critical, constructive, and comprehensive?

Another example of an assessment method that illustrates consistent attention to a teaching philosophy also illustrates how a teaching philosophy can be implemented in a curricular or programmatic fashion. When Erlene was graduate program director, she collaborated with faculty to institute a writing initiative throughout the curriculum (Grise-Owens, Drury, Rickman, 2017; Grise-Owens & Crum, 2012; Miller, et al., in press). This programmatic change was initiated because of teaching philosophies that embraced a professional communication emphasis. Most students struggled with writing, a core professional communication competency. An empowering approach was to provide students with the resources to succeed.

A key element of the writing initiative was for all incoming students to take a professional writing course (Grise-Owens & Crum, 2012), which introduced students to a standard writing rubric that was used throughout the curriculum. A standardized rubric conveys consistent standards and provides consistent feedback, which promotes more student engagement and deeper learning (Grise-Owens & Crum; Stevens & Levi, 2005). As noted earlier, students also complete a PDP, identifying specific areas and strategies for improving their writing. The writing rubric gives them a familiar framework for that assignment. Likewise, the course takes a holistic approach to developing the professional skill of writing. Thus, students have assignments that assess their attention to the cognitive and affective aspects of the writing process along with knowledge and skill development (Grise-Owens, Drury, Rickman, 2017; Miller et al., in press; Pyles & Adam, 2016).

Another example of implementing a teaching philosophy uses an assessment method across a curriculum. In a graduate program where Erlene was the MSW director, Jay initiated a licensing preparatory initiative across the curriculum (Miller, Grise-Owens, & Escobar-Ratliff, 2015). Several faculty members participated in the initiative. The initiative had several components, including specific workshops for students on how to take the licensing exam. In terms of assessment, faculty members incorporated quizzes into courses throughout the program; typically, these quizzes assessed comprehension and application of assigned readings. Specifically, these quizzes mirrored the format of the professional licensing exam. In keeping with our teaching philosophy, syllabi included the following rationale for this assignment: "The MSW program is committed to supporting students in preparation for professional licensing upon graduation. Thus, the exam question format will mimic the CSW exam format and will contribute to students' self-efficacy in test-taking." This assessment mode implemented our teaching philosophy emphases, such as encompassing and relevant application.

This implementation through attention to culture, assignments, and assessment is specifically connected to the teaching philosophy shared in the first class. As the previous discussion illustrates, your teaching philosophy provides a foundational basis for, and is an explicit theme or thread in, all aspects of the teaching–learning experience. The philosophy is implemented through the class culture, tasks, assignments, assessments, and outcomes. Implementing a teaching philosophy requires consistency, congruence, and intentionality. Inherently, being intentional about using the teaching philosophy, and sharing that philosophy in the learning community, requires the instructor to be vulnerable, flexible, and open to critical feedback pertaining to the philosophy. Commitment to the congruence and consistency of the teaching philosophy requires the philosophy to be organic, fluid and growing.

In implementing a teaching philosophy, we must ensure our assessment methods are consistent with our teaching philosophy. Likewise, activation of the philosophy requires an intentional, ongoing evaluation of how we enact the teaching philosophy itself. In the next chapter, we discuss key considerations related to the evaluation of your philosophy and provide pragmatic strategies for how to meet this aim.

Chapter 5

OK! I'm Implementing My Philosophy: How Do I Evaluate It?

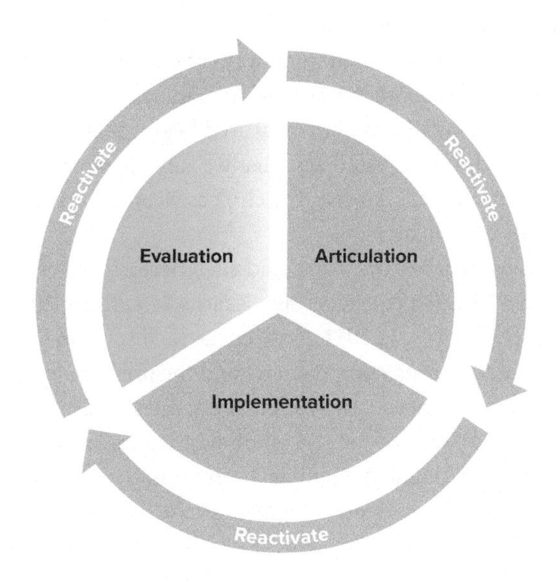

Throughout this book, we have discussed the crucial importance of a grounded and engaged philosophy for adept and engaged teaching and learning. In the preceding chapters, we fashioned an approach to guide you through articulating and implementing your teaching-learning philosophy. This chapter focuses on an often neglected component of the teaching philosophy—evaluation. We discuss four key elements of evaluation including (a) valuing evaluation, (b) conceptualizing your evaluation approach, (c) executing your evaluation approach, and (d) responding to and using feedback.

As we emphasized in the earlier chapters, we provide universally applicable strategies and ideas, not a template. We integrate examples from our practice to illustrate key points. You need to adapt the information and examples provided to your philosophy and context.

Valuing Evaluation

First, we want to clarify what we mean by evaluation and why it is essential for an activated philosophy. Evaluation is an analysis to determine whether a certain set of actions met specified goals (Krysik & Finn, 2013). Knowles, Holton, and Swanson (2005) said that the key query associated with evaluation in teaching and learning is "What systematic collection of evidence needs to be carried out to determine whether my desired changes took place" (p. 179). This "desired change," as they suggest, refers to meeting your teaching–learning goals, or in other words actualizing your philosophy.

In Chapter 3 we emphasized the need for reflecting on values as an integral part of articulation. Similarly, activating the evaluation aspect of your teaching philosophy involves critically reflecting on the value of evaluation. We also need to critically consider what our evaluation conveys about what we value. That is, to paraphrase a common maxim, we measure what matters.

We would add to that maxim: What's measured begins to matter more. The articulation of our philosophy crystallizes what we value in teaching and learning and what we want to promote. Likewise, the choices we make about evaluation shows what we value, what matters.

Broad consensus emphasizes the value, and even necessity, of evaluating teaching philosophies (Buskist & Davis 2006; Kearns & Sullivan, 2011; Reber, 2011; Royse 2001; Schussler et al., 2011). Indeed, as we discuss in Chapter 6, the growing emphasis on evaluating competencies and the pressure for institutional accountability reinforce this need (Alexander, 2000; Anastas, 2010; CSWE, 2015; Huisman & Currie, 2004) Yet, for one reason or another, the evaluation of one's philosophy seems to be an ongoing quandary—and missing link—in higher education. Although evaluation is an "integral and crucial" component of teaching and learning (Fox, 2013, p. 145), many educators still find evaluative assessment challenging (Anastas, 2010; Fink, 2003; Fox, 2013; Walvoord & Anderson, 1998). Alexander et al. (2012) described the evaluation of a philosophy as a "layer of complexity" (p. 24). Chism (1998) expressed a similar notion. Ambiguity related to evaluation models and metrics, competing academic priorities, and a lack of a clearly articulated philosophy are but a few of the factors that may impede efforts necessary to evaluate your philosophy.

Although challenging, we need to be clear: Evaluation is a vital component of an actualized teaching philosophy. Let's face it, adroit educational practices require significant ingenuity and investment, and in most (if not all) instances, the quality of education is inherently connected to the quality of individuals in a given profession or discipline. Given this investment, and the impact of this investment on students, we as educators need to know if the way we apply our teaching and learning is effective.

Teaching philosophies parallel our engagement of learning, that is, the interactive evidence of education. How can we expect our students to engage effectively in learning if we do not invest, examine, and evaluate our teaching? How do we ensure that we as educators demonstrate competent practice? How do we know that we are consistently modeling, mentoring, and mirroring (Fox, 2013) what we want students to learn? Throughout this book, we advocate that an activated teaching–learning philosophy is essential for the purposes of effective and significant teaching and learning. Indeed, as Weimer (2002) appositely suggested, it "makes no sense" (p. 187) not to evaluate your teaching and learning. Now that we see the value of evaluation, let's make sense and figure out how to evaluate what our teaching philosophies say we value and then how to use that evaluation.

Conceptualizing Your Evaluation Approach

Emphatically, apt and effective evaluation starts with explicit attention to articulating your philosophy (see Chapter 3) and having a clear plan for implementing the philosophy (see Chapter 4). However, even if you have a clearly articulated and appropriately implemented philosophy, evaluation can still prove challenging. Conceptualizing an evaluation approach must be intentional and informed and it needs to be integrally connected with articulation and implementation, contrasted with just being an afterthought. In other words, as you articulate your philosophy and plan ways to put it into action, you need to consider how you will assess whether the implementation is congruent and effective. As with articulation and implementation, give attention to diversity, power, and privilege. For instance, do your evaluative modalities capture diverse input, balance power dynamics, and offset hegemonic perspectives?

The questions we ask determine the answers we seek. Thus, the framing of the questions for evaluation are critically important. When it comes to your philosophy, evaluation is not simply examining the paradoxical question, Is my teaching philosophy good? Framing the question in this manner is limiting and unclear, and trying to definitively answer that query is largely an exercise in futility. Instead, we advocate more meaningful purpose and useful aims for evaluation, which can be achieved through a holistic, multimodal, evaluative approach that takes into account multiple perspectives. Such an approach moves beyond assessing such limited criterion as participation in a course or satisfaction with the course materials or instructor to evaluating learning impact and outcomes.

Within this frame, key questions include, How do I know my philosophy is congruent with best pedagogical and andragogical practices? How is my philosophy creating an environment conducive to teaching and learning for all participants?

How do I assess the activities and strategies I identified as implementing my philosophy? How will I use the information gleaned from this evaluation to deepen learning? How will I use this information to further activate my philosophy? Next, we discuss how to begin to explore some of these questions.

First, critically consider evaluative methods already in place. In most instances, your teaching has been, is, or will be assessed by standard course evaluations. Typically these types of evaluations are administered to students, usually on completion of a course. Although these summative evaluations can certainly have utilitarian functions, several people have expressed cautions related to their use. For instance, Weimer (1993) said the formal end-of-course evaluations are usually simply used to "make good personnel decisions" (p. 114) for the institution and that this limited use can "comprise their effectiveness" (Weimer, 2011, p. 50). In some sense, these evaluations can become more about popularity (i.e., Do you like the instructor?), than about assessing the impact of teaching–learning activities (although those factors do not have to be mutually exclusive).

Consider ways to make these summative evaluations more directly related to evaluating your teaching philosophy. For example, Erlene links items on this evaluation with aspects of her teaching philosophy. For instance, an item on the university evaluation that asks about availability of the professor links to the encompassing tenet of her philosophy, which is mentoring students beyond the classroom and seeing the faculty role as encouraging professional development. In promotion, tenure, and academic reviews, you can discuss these linkages and use them to evaluate your effectiveness through the lens of your philosophy.

Another typical way faculty members think about conceptualizing evaluation approaches is how evaluation applies to students (Anastas, 2010; Weimer, 2002). Ordinarily, when it comes to evaluation faculty members think about grading, the types of grades students receive, and how those grades may reflect on their teaching. Certainly, grades can be useful in assessing your philosophy. However, focusing solely on grading may not fully capture all elements of your philosophy or may present a skewed view of the impact of your philosophy.

Although multifarious, the purposes of evaluating your teaching and learning are inherently connected (Anastas, 2010; Fink, 2003). In some instances, evaluation will be used for personal and professional growth and development. Another function may be associated with the aforementioned personnel decisions, and some evaluation metrics may be used to select teaching awards and recognitions. Ultimately, for an activated philosophy, you want to use evaluation to gauge the merit and applicability of your philosophy in promoting effective teaching and learning.

Given this array of functions, your evaluation approach should be multifaceted. In conceptualizing your evaluation approach, we recommend taking into account five *C*s: congruency, context, clarity, comprehensiveness, and commitment.

Perhaps paramount to the conceptualization of your philosophy evaluation approach is the element of congruency. Is your evaluation approach congruent with your philosophy? For example, if you adhere to a criticalist type of philosophy, does your evaluation approach mirror these beliefs? Is the philosophy congruent with best (and evolving) educational practices? For example, as we discussed earlier, tenets of the flipped classroom are congruent with our philosophies, which emphasize active learning (Lang, 2017). Viewing the primary function of evaluation as ensuring a paralleled congruency will serve you well in evaluating the impact of your philosophy.

Of course, realistically, what you do will be influenced by the context in which you do it. As Walvoord and Anderson (1998) postulated, all teaching and learning, and any associated evaluation of that teaching and learning, is "context-specific" (p. 149). Every class, every institution, every learning community is nuanced. Evaluation approaches must take into account these nuanced contextual factors (Fox, 2013). Considerations should be given to class size, platform (online, hybrid, and so forth), and institution type (e.g., research, teaching, public, private, and so forth), among other factors. For example, in Chapter 6 Erlene describes leading an MSW program's change to a hybrid platform and the application of her philosophy to that format.

Next, clarity as it relates to constructing an evaluation approach is essential. In evaluating your philosophy, you need to clearly operationalize outcomes. This operationalization means being clear about what you want to achieve, the mode you will use to assess this achievement, and the standard that will define success in meeting teaching–learning outcomes.

The evaluation approach needs to be comprehensive as well as clear. Reviewing the literature on evaluation may be misleading, as much of it frames evaluation as pertaining to a single course. However, this frame is a limited conception of evaluation as it applies to your philosophy. Evaluation of your philosophy should entail a comprehensive approach, which includes using formative and summative assessment strategies as well as incorporating multiple perspectives over time. This comprehensive approach includes examining class assignments, meetings, and teaching–learning objectives more broadly. In Chapter 4 we emphasize that the implementation of your philosophy involves every aspect of your teaching from syllabi to class environment to assignments, assessments, and so forth, and not just in one course, rather across courses. Stepping back and examining your philosophy in this way will allow a more holistic examination of strengths and opportunities for growth.

Finally, attention to congruency, context, clarity, and comprehensiveness, requires commitment. Bain (2004) said that educators must be committed to ongoing evaluation. We certainly concur with this belief. Evaluation can be difficult, and you must be committed to the ongoing execution of evaluation and iterative usage of the feedback gleaned from that evaluation.

Executing Your Evaluation Approach

In discussing the importance of execution, famed business consultant Tim Berry (2015) said that "planning is nine parts execution, and one part strategy" (para. 3). Although Berry's proportions may be debatable, the importance of execution is not debatable. Execution is carrying out a planned course of action. Once conceptualized, executing your evaluation plan is the first step in assessing whether your philosophy is meeting the intended goals.

Although considerable attention is given to promulgating advice on good teaching–learning experiences, fewer resources are available for how one should execute an evaluation plan (Brookfield, 2015). A deft approach to evaluation of your philosophy requires collecting feedback from multiple constituencies. Holistic evaluation approaches require such a practice. Next, we discuss considerations and strategies for executing your evaluation plan, not by approach but rather by the potential stakeholder providing the information and, through dissemination, receiving the feedback from evaluations. These constituents include oneself, students, colleagues, university administration, and the broader teaching–learning community.

In earlier chapters, especially when discussing articulation, we emphasize the importance of self-reflection. This emphasis is echoed either explicitly or implicitly in any discussion about effective teaching and learning (Bain, 2004; Fox, 2013; hooks, 2003; Parker, 1998; Vella, 2002). Likewise, the importance of critical self-reflection for the purposes of evaluation cannot be overstated (Brookfield, 2015). We concur with Weimer's (1993) assertion that you as an educator are in the best place to know about your teaching. As we discuss in previous chapters, developing a philosophy is a highly personal endeavor. So, too, is the process of evaluating the impact of that philosophy.

In the helping professions, such as social work, the concept of professional use of self has long been recognized as an invaluable tool in assessing one's own professional practice (Fox, 2003; Maclean, 2010). This use of self can manifest itself through reflexive practice, which is a form of critical self-analysis that serves to improve competence (Biggs, 1999; Clouder, 2000). Several authors discussed the importance of critical self-reflection (Fook, & Askeland, 2007; Theobald, Gardner, & Long, 2017) and the use of what is often called *reflexive practice*, which means to reflect for the purpose of changing actions (Lay & McGuire, 2010; Hickson, 2011). Traditional educationalists, such as Dewey (1933), discussed the significance of reflecting on experiences as a tool for learning. McKeachie (2002) asserted that this type of self-assessment is a "potential resource for continued growth—perhaps the most important of all" (p. 332). McCormack and Kennelly (2011) suggested that although knowledge about self-reflection and reflexive practice is not widely known in educational contexts, it is a valuable approach for assessing teaching practices. Reber (2011) provided a multistep process for assessing a teaching philosophy, much of which focuses on self-reflection, and suggested reflecting on the underlying assumptions of teaching and learning as well as examining students' philosophies of teaching and learning. Seldin & Associates, (1993) suggested that the very purpose of developing a philosophy is to foster the encouragement of reflection. Others have expressed the importance of reflection in the context of education (Drolet, 2013; Fink, 2003; Fitzmaurice, 2008; Kearns & Sullivan, 2011; Schussler et al., 2011; Wang, 2012).

Engaging in critical self-reflection is an integral approach to evaluating your philosophy, but this practice does not have to be only an exercise in sequestered meditation. A number of tools can aid in this reflection for evaluation purposes. For instance, the Teaching Perspectives Inventory can be a helpful device for reflectively assessing your philosophy (Pratt & Collins, 2002). This tool assesses self-reported data related to five contrasting views of constructs associated with teaching. According to Collins and Pratt (2011), this tool can be used "in aiding self-reflection" and assessing your teaching–learning (p. 358).

As mentioned in our discussion of using reflection to articulate your philosophy, you can adapt reflective practice models that do not specifically pertain to teaching. Maclean (2010) provides an accessible summary of several models to guide reflection. Borton (1970) described a reflective practice model that focuses on three queries: What? So what? And now what? This simple approach can be a good start to examining your philosophy. For example, you can identify what articulated aspect of your philosophy you want to evaluate and through what implemented measure (e.g., assignment, environmental factors, and so forth). Then, you can test the congruence between them: So what does the information from this implementation really tell you? Then reflect on now what will you do with that information—adjust the assignment, adapt your philosophy, share collected feedback with constituents, and so forth.

Other strategies to aid in self-reflection may include recording and reviewing instructional exercises (Fox, 2013; Weimer, 1993), undertaking autoethnographic endeavors (Chang & Boyd, 2011; Hickson, 2011), and traditional journal keeping (McKeachie, 2002), among others. The processes we describe in Chapter 3 for guiding the articulation of your philosophy can be looped in with evaluative measures. Again, the articulation, implementation, and evaluation of your philosophy is an iterative and interactive process, contrasted with separate and nonrelated phases.

In addition to self-reflection, students and the feedback they offer are pivotal in assessing your philosophy. As noted previously, a commonly used assessment output of teaching and learning is student grades. A host of authors have discussed student grading and ample resources aimed at assisting educators in practices associated with grading. Walvoord and Anderson (2010) provide one of the most comprehensive resources for improving grading practices and discuss the use of grading for evaluation purposes for faculty and institutions.

We want to stress the importance of student input, grades, and so forth. Grades can certainly be important instruments used to evaluate your philosophy because they provide solid input. But grades are simply a piece of information, not the piece of information. As McKeachie (2002) aptly stated, "Evaluation is a great deal more than giving a grade" (p. 103). Relying on grades alone is not a sufficient way to evaluate your philosophy.

Interestingly, educators seldom involve students in constructing the learning environment. More specifically, students are rarely provided with an opportunity to evaluate instructors' fulfillment of their philosophy except when being assessed for particular assignments (e.g., graded) and responding to an end-of-course evaluation. We advocate for educators to involve students in all aspects of the educational experience. This perception is certainly congruent with other perspectives presented in the literature. In discussing student involvement, as we emphasized in discussing implementing your philosophy, we advocate for students to have the opportunity to make recommendations about all aspects of the course. Actively engaging students in teaching and learning, including the evaluation of your philosophy, will contribute to developing a healthy educational environment suitable for adroit teaching and learning (Fox, 2013; Roche et al., 1999).

Involving students in the evaluation of your philosophy should occur at the outset of any course and in an ongoing fashion (Anastas, 2010; Weimer, 2002; Vella, 2002). This involvement includes involving students in setting course decorum and norms, assignments, and the assessment tools used to evaluate learning outcomes and subsequently your philosophy. This engagement can be achieved a variety of ways.

For instance, at the beginning of every course, Jay sends out a draft of the course syllabus and gives students the opportunity to complete a Syllabus Review Worksheet. This exercise allows students the opportunity to provide feedback about assignments, course objectives, and assessment mechanisms. Additionally, the review sheet asks students to reflect on elements of the course they perceive will contribute the most or least to their learning and the outcomes they hope to achieve. During the first class session, Jay uses this information to negotiate course parameters, activities, and outcomes. In turn this feedback is used to evaluate aspects of his philosophy.

Student involvement in contributing to the evaluation of your philosophy should not be limited to the start of a course; rather, this involvement should occur throughout the course. Larry takes a formative approach to assessing his philosophy at the midpoint of each of his courses. As noted in the discussion on articulation, Larry shares his teaching philosophy with students at the beginning of the course. Then at midpoint he administers formal surveys that include scaled and open-ended items designed to collect primary data from students about their experiences in the course up to that point. He explicitly provides the students with his philosophy statement again and asks questions to assess to what level and in what ways he enacts his philosophy. This type of approach offers several distinct benefits.

Conducting an assessment at midterm allows Larry to identify areas of concern before the class ends, and Larry is able to address student concerns while it is still relevant to the students providing the feedback. This is a benefit not available to instructors who rely on the typical end-of-course evaluations. In keeping with Larry's philosophical tenet of relevant application, this use of evaluation models for students the importance of evaluation in the assessment of professional practice. Larry uses the documentation of the formative and summative evaluations in his annual reviews and promotion and tenure portfolio.

In another example of a formative approach, in a program where Erlene taught, courses met for extended four-hour class sessions every other week-end. As a hybrid format, the program also had online class sessions. After each class, the students completed a brief formative evaluation, and in the next class session the faculty member would provide a composite of that feedback and discuss any matters that needed attention. Erlene used this discussion to clarify and reinforce connections to her teaching philosophy (e.g., purpose of particular assignments, attention to class environment, and so forth). Notably, as a class exercise for learning about developing practice evaluation instruments, students assessed the evaluation and formulated an update to the evaluation form.

Erlene linked items on this formative evaluation with each of the tenets of her teaching philosophy. For instance, she used the item "I felt free to participate" as one measure of the empowering tenet. This ongoing formative assessment provided a clear, consistent way to comprehensively assess the congruence of her philosophy in the context. Through commitment to ongoing evaluation, she could track this assessment over time. In promotion and tenure and annual reviews, she discussed the use of this evaluation.

In addition to these examples, where students are concerned, the evaluation of your teaching philosophy can take many additional forms. Several authors have discussed the use of standardized instruments as a mechanism for evaluating teaching philosophies. For example, Jay uses a formal self-care practice scale to assess student competency for a multidisciplinary self-care course. Erlene used a critical thinking scale to evaluate learning outcomes in some of her courses. Other useful scales include the Critical Incident Questionnaire (Brookfield, 2015), and the Student-Instructor Relationship Scale (Creasey, Jarvis, & Knapcik, 2009), among others. Again, consider your particular philosophy's tenets, then look for scales or other instruments that might be pertinent to evaluate them.

As with any evaluative tool, it is important for standardized tools to not be used in isolation. Although undoubtedly useful, Brookfield (2015) expressed the need to be cautious about the use of such instruments and that educators should not see these types of evaluative tools as a panacea for assessing the teaching philosophy. Rather, he said, these tools are simply "one assessment approach among many" (p. 195).

Of course, we would be remiss if we didn't provide a note of caution. In implementing your evaluation approach, you want to ensure that participants in the learning community are protected ethically and otherwise. This protection includes being sensitive to data collection approaches, uses of data, confidentiality, and so forth. This protection starts with creating a learning environment in which students feel comfortable and being respectful and cautious with any feedback you wish them to provide. Not being attentive to ethical considerations may lead to counterproductivity as it relates to meeting your teaching–learning goals.

Next, without question, your colleagues can be an asset in the evaluation of your philosophy. Peer feedback has long been recognized as pertinent to many fields of human industry, and education is no different. Surely, as Weimer (1993) postulated, as an educator you "need to engage colleagues in efforts to understand and improve instruction" (p. 119).

Foundationally, it is imperative for educators to engage in critical dialogue with peers about teaching and learning. Gibbs, Knapper, and Picinnin (2007) discussed the importance of critical dialogue among peers about learning. However, despite this importance, "reflective conversations have all but disappeared from everyday academic practice" (McCormack & Kennelly, 2011, p. 515).

Thus, educators must intentionally seek to engage in critical discourse about teaching and learning. As we discuss in Chapter 6, fostering a teaching–learning culture includes involving peers in more structured activities, such as the development of formal learning communities, book clubs, and teaching–learning retreats. Less formal approaches, such as setting time aside after faculty meetings or the proverbial hallway meeting can be useful. Ultimately, being intentional about engaging peers in critical dialogue about teaching and learning in general and about your philosophy specifically will assist you in thinking more deeply about your philosophy. As Knowles, Holton, and Swanson (2005) said, peers can be among the "richest resources" in teaching and learning (p. 66).

The use of peers in the evaluation of your philosophy should extend beyond critical dialogue. For instance, although some literature has cautioned about the limitations of peer observations in teaching (Weimer, 2002), peer feedback from observations can be a valuable component to improving your teaching and learning (Anastas, 2010; Bain, 2004). We have found that observations can be a useful tool. Larry's program has a structured peer observation system in which tenured faculty observe in courses of untenured faculty. The observing faculty member completes a standardized form, which is shared with the faculty member being observed. Larry used these observations in his promotion and tenure documents. Similarly, as we discuss in Chapter 6, team teaching can offer an excellent in vivo opportunity for evaluation.

An important caveat about engaging peers in the evaluation of your philosophy is to seek peers who provide feedback in a critical but collegial way. Especially for any ongoing purposes of evaluation, this peer should be someone with whom you have a trusting relationship (McKeachie, 2002), or as the literature on reflective practice calls it, a critical friend (Stenhouse, 1975). A critical friend is willing to listen carefully, support, challenge, and ask questions to "prompt deeper thinking" (Maclean, 2010, p. 72). Being a critical friend is advantageous as well because it develops reflective practice skills (Dahlgren, et al, 2006). Having confidence in your colleagues' ability to provide thoughtful, considerate feedback is imperative to building an ethos of collegial support and in turn providing insight useful in the evaluation of teaching. We can attest that having each other and other colleagues as critical friends improves our professional work and our human spirits.

In a broader sense, peer evaluation can come from active engagement with the SoTL community, which can take the form of attending and presenting at conferences, participating in webinars, or reading books with an interactive approach. Finally, as we mentioned at the outset of this section, consider ways to use university-wide and administrative-driven formats of evaluation. Connecting those formats, in conjunction with self, student, and peer evaluative input gives you a multifaceted approach.

If you are reading this book in an interactive fashion, you are engaging in a form of peer evaluation. Congratulations! Be sure to document this process and how it affects your teaching and learning in your PDP, annual review, and promotion and tenure documents.

Responding to and Using Feedback

When engaging in evaluation, keep three things in mind. First, as we noted earlier, be certain and clear about the questions you are asking; second, if you ask a question, you may find an answer; and third, that answer may not be the one you were expecting.

First, we want to emphasize the nuanced but crucial difference in responding to feedback versus reacting. That is, no matter the evaluative approach, you must put yourself in a space to be receptive and responsive, not defensive. Being responsive, as contrasted with reacting, allows you to critically assess feedback and constructively use the feedback to make necessary adaptations. In some cases these changes may involve being clearer with yourself and others about the tenets of your philosophy. In other cases, it may involve making changes to assignments, classroom environment, and so forth.

Unfortunately, many educators do not appropriately respond to negative feedback about their instruction. Weimer (2011) said that faculty often overreact to negative evaluative feedback. In discussing his own experiences, Brookfield (2015) said his first impulse when receiving negative feedback is to "react emotionally" (p. 197).

As authors we have certainly had our share of unexpected feedback. Jay recounts his experience receiving course evaluations from the first social work practice class he ever taught in the following:

> I thought the class went really well. We all laughed a lot and had fun. I thought the students really grasped the concepts. Turns out, I was wrong. I got the feedback from the University course evaluation and the students thought differently. The questions about actual learning were rated really low. I vividly recall a comment in which one student thought the course was "fun"—but also reported that they "didn't learn much." I was devastated. I found myself both mad and sad. It was really disheartening.

Of course, no educator wants to receive negative feedback. No one wants to learn that his or her teaching approaches fell short of meeting a specified outcome. However, it is important for you to see these experiences as normative. As an engaged educator, you will undoubtedly try new approaches, activities, and assignments. Trying new things means you will learn new things. Instead of viewing negative feedback, shall we say, negatively, we recommend reframing any feedback as an opportunity to improve your teaching and learning. Jay reframed this experience as important input and made specific changes in the next class, such as asking the students for feedback earlier (e.g., midterm) so that perceived deficits could be addressed.

In another example of reframing, several years ago Erlene exuberantly reported to a colleague about an enjoyable teaching experience in a practice course in which the students engaged deeply in a learning exercise. Then, wearily and defensively, Erlene said, "But, then they started complaining about writing!" The astute colleague (aka critical friend) queried, "Well, were they *complaining* or were they *commenting*?" This reframing made Erlene pause and reflect. Fortuitously, the next class included the topic of how to handle resistance in our social work practice. Operating from her teaching philosophy, Erlene used the example of her experiencing their input as resistance in a negative way. Then, she recounted how the interchange with her colleague challenged that interpretation.

This example illustrates the importance of being intentional about viewing input, including resistance, as commentary to be addressed collaboratively versus complaints that set up an adversarial dynamic (Kilmer, 2007). Notably, this interchange provided a playful yet productive norm for the class. Students would in good spirit preface challenging input by saying, "We are not complaining. We are commenting." Likewise, Erlene was more able to hear their input, assess it on merits, and have collaborative responses. Rather than just responding defensively, this approach allows us to use any feedback for improvement.

Ultimately, evaluation of a teaching philosophy requires being vulnerable (hooks, 2003; Palmer, 1998). Weimer (1993) said that "much like students who get personally involved in assessments of their learning, it is easy for teachers to feel the same vulnerabilities when it comes to assessments of their instruction" (p. 114). We choose to name and embrace that vulnerability, and we suggest you do the same. Discussing this vulnerability openly with students and colleagues alike will give you the ability to more effectively receive critical feedback about your philosophy and use it to constructively refine your teaching.

One of the ways we embrace that vulnerability is through modeling. As noted earlier, we typically discuss formative feedback with the class, which at times is negative or problematic. We strive to model our teaching philosophies and mirror professional principles. Similarly, we routinely share with students some of the feedback that we have received as part of our professional roles. Students seem particularly intrigued when we share our experiences of negative feedback on our writing, such as reviews of submitted manuscripts. This shared experience of receiving feedback that may be difficult to receive promotes a sense of commonality and humility in the teaching–learning process.

As part of this vulnerability and using all input for evaluative purposes, we caution you to be cognizant of the impact of the consumeristic environment in which education occurs (Barber, 2007; Gottfried, 2002). In this context, students (and faculty) may be accustomed to operating in what Freire (1998, 2007a, 2007b) famously dubbed the *banking model* in which students pay their money and then presume that the customer is always right. In this banking, consumeristic model, students pay their money for the guarantee of a degree, not necessarily an education; the student is treated as a customer using a service, rather than a learner being challenged (Gottfried, 2002; Miller & Grise-Owens, 2008). Regrettably, much of the educational system reinforces this customer satisfaction model. So, if your teaching philosophy, as ours does, involves challenging students to think critically and engage in the learning process, you may receive resistance and negativity. Palmer aptly described this phenomenon:

> Good education may leave students deeply dissatisfied. I do not mean the dissatisfaction that comes from [incompetent faculty]. But, students who have been well served by good teachers may walk away angry that their prejudices have been challenged and their sense of self shaken. (p. 94)

In the banking, consumeristic model, this dissatisfaction would be assessed as failure. However, Palmer further asserted, "That sort of dissatisfaction may be a sign that real education has happened" (p. 94).

This dynamic is so important (and, yet complex) that we hope examples from our practice will illuminate. Operating from her teaching philosophy of engaging diversity, Erlene explicitly challenges White male privilege in her classes. Not surprisingly, over the years White male students have responded with anger and dissatisfaction. This response from students is difficult to traverse. However, with practice, Erlene has learned to be intentional about owning her vulnerability, framing the situation more neutrally, relying on colleagues for support, and focusing on the learning. This approach promotes interacting with the students experiencing this dissatisfaction in a way that promotes shared growth. Actually, alumni report that these interchanges are some of the most significant learning experiences in content and process. (Erlene's epitaph shall read: It's *all* about the learning!)

Similarly, particularly in his social policy courses, Larry receives feedback from students about his "liberal political views." In his reflection on this feedback, Larry is informed by the SoTL literature. As Caughie (2007) and Kilmer (2007) clarified, teaching is a form of advocating particular values such as valuing evidence, embracing professional standards, and so forth. For example, the NASW (2017) promulgates values for the profession, which competent social workers are required to enact. With his teaching philosophy tenet of relevant application, Larry clarifies the relevance of his assertions and challenges in class in the context of social work's professional principles, practices, and purposes. He models critical thinking skills through providing information and leading discussions that challenge assumptions. For example, with his global emphasis, he uses global comparisons. Again, students may be dissatisfied by this challenge of their belief systems. However, in terms of his teaching philosophy's aim of preparing competent practitioners, he can know that "real education has happened" (Parker, 1998, p. 94).

As we noted earlier, reflection is an important aspect of using evaluation. Part of this reflection involves considering the cultural context of input and how to navigate that culture in a manner that remains true to your philosophy. Although done on an individual basis, this type of reflection is significantly enhanced by dialogue with critical friends and the broader SoTL community.

This contextual reflection can be informed by research on the critique of the merits, efficacy, and usefulness, as well as limitations and possible biases in evaluation. Fortunately, as part of the SoTL literature, this critical research is growing. For example, increasingly researchers explore the oftentimes biased relationship between evaluation results and diverse social identities such as race, ethnicity, gender, gender identity, sexual orientation, age, and so forth (Aruguete, Slater, & Mwaikinda, 2017; Boring, 2017; Jennings, 2010; Kogan, Schoenfeld-Tacher, & Hellyer, 2010; Lawrence, 2018; Smith, 2009; Stonebraker & Stone, 2015; Storage, Home, Cimpian, & Leslie, 2016; Wagner, Rieger, & Voorvelt, 2016).

Flaherty (2018) reported that some universities are looking for ways to offset the increasingly documented problems of bias as well as the propensity for student evaluations to be popularity contests. For example, the University of Southern California quit using student evaluations of teaching (SET) data in promotion and tenure decisions. SETs continue to be available for students to complete; faculty are expected to explain in their portfolios how they use student feedback. However, the actual data are not used in promotion and tenure processes; instead, the emphasis is on faculty peer evaluation. Flaherty cites another example, the University of Oregon, which is eliminating traditional SETs and instead implementing a Continuous Improvement and Evaluation of Teaching Systems. This holistic approach includes multiple formative and summative evaluative elements, including student input.

Attention to bias and consumeristic pressures (e.g., grade inflation, popularity contests, student or customer satisfaction) is crucial. Concomitantly, as we discussed earlier, critical use of student feedback is an important way of assessing one's teaching in general and one's teaching–learning philosophy specifically. Flaherty (2018) recommends a balanced evaluative approach: Find or develop SETs that are well designed to limit bias such as using questions that focus on learning and student engagement contrasted with rate my professor; use all evaluation data critically including watching for patterns over time, interpreting contextually, adjusting for bias, and ignoring irrelevant data; and use multiple sources of data, including peer evaluations, course artifacts, and self-evaluations along with student perspectives from SETs.

The following are a couple of key reminders about the use of student feedback. First, especially early in your career, seek support or advice in responding to feedback.

In addition to self-reflection, use team teaching, critical friends, and mentors to gain perspective. For example, early in her career, Erlene received a sharply negative comment on an evaluation. Reactively, she focused on that comment, which seemed personalized. Fortunately, Erlene shared this feedback with a seasoned colleague, who said, "Oh, yeah! That's [Name of student]. She says that in everybody's class." Her colleague said, "When looking at feedback, you need to look at the entire evaluation. Actually, you need to look across courses. That comment is an outlier. Instead, let's look at the themes." That collegial advice helped Erlene refocus on responding to the feedback more productively rather than reacting personally.

Similarly, examine the feedback in the context where you teach. For example, a couple of students conveyed their displeasure that Larry does not offer extra credit. On further exploration, Larry realized that most faculty where he taught offered extra credit. (The program did not have a formal policy.) Therefore, Larry was not following the norm. With this student critique, Larry faced a dilemma, either change his policy to fit the norm or continue to adhere to his policy. Based on his philosophy, he decided to adhere to a no extra credit policy, and he is more intentional about explaining his rationale for that policy to students. Also, he recognizes that students have the right to comment on their dislike of that policy. At the same time, some students report liking the fairness of the no extra credit policy. Ultimately, student learning, not just student satisfaction, is the goal. He discusses these contextual considerations in his evaluation documents.

This discussion about the use of feedback magnifies the need for activating a teaching philosophy. An activated philosophy engages contextual considerations, reflective analysis, and systematic critique. As universities move toward more holistic approaches to assessing teaching, an activated philosophy offers an ideal framework for interpreting and using all forms of evaluation.

Finally, we want to discuss use of feedback through dissemination of information from your evaluation. Many may not think about the evaluative function of dissemination. Typically, dissemination is viewed as the traditional scholarship (e.g., publications and presentations) associated with research endeavors, but through the lens of SoTL, disseminating the evaluation of your philosophy is a research endeavor. Furthermore, dissemination allows you to receive additional feedback from the constituents—students, colleagues, and the broader academic community.

In essence, dissemination is the strategic distribution of pertinent information to constituents. The goal of dissemination is to develop new insights and knowledge related to a particular area of inquiry that have the potential to shape (or reshape) future actions (Yale Center for Clinical Investigation, n.d.).

One of the first steps in any dissemination plan is ensuring that the results are made available to the participants. In terms of your philosophy, a primary constituent group is undoubtedly students. Sharing your evaluation approach and subsequent findings with students can convey that you (a) value input, (b) put your philosophy into practice, and (c) model best practices of using evaluation to inform practice.

Likewise, it is best practice to disseminate results associated with your philosophy to broader academic audiences, which may be achieved in several ways. First, disseminate your evaluation efforts to the university administration, which ensures you are working smarter and smarter. Use the documentation of the activation of your philosophy in your faculty evaluative processes, such as annual evaluations, promotion and tenure processes, professional development plans, and so forth.

Second, as we emphasize throughout the book, involvement with SoTL communities can be beneficial in achieving feedback about your work. Sharing your works formally in SoTL forums not only provides an outlet for professional development but serves as a primary arena for receiving feedback. As we stated earlier, we participate in a number of these conferences and present works pertaining to the activation of our teaching philosophies. As shown in our examples throughout the book, we develop SoTL products from critical attention to myriad aspects of our teaching, from assignments to environment to assessment. This active participation in and contribution to SoTL was the impetus for this book.

Dissemination allows you to garner information specifically related to the evaluation of your philosophy, which feeds your professional development. In turn, this use of evaluation refines how you articulate and implement your philosophy. Thus, your philosophy is activated. But, it is not a finished product. Rather, as we discuss in the next chapter, an activated philosophy must be sustained over time. ■

Chapter 6

And, Reactivate!

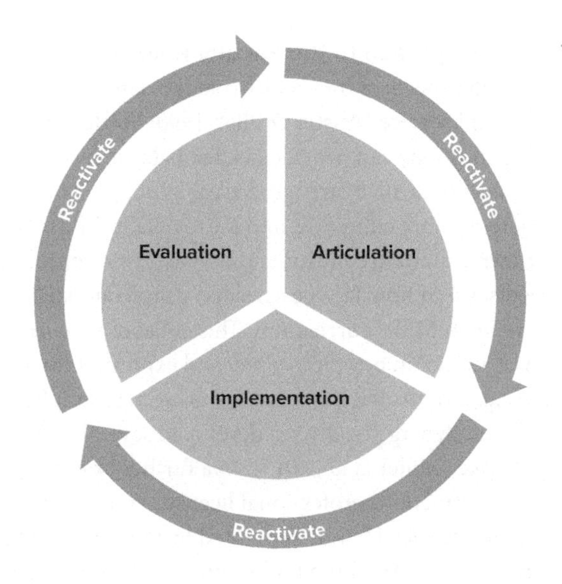

As we have emphasized throughout the book, an activated philosophy is not a one-and-done task. Rather, it is a dynamic, ongoing process. An organic philosophy is the core of sustaining passion for teaching and ensuring competence in fostering learning (Owens, Miller, & Grise-Owens, 2014). This final chapter discusses the exponential effect of continual reactivation of a philosophy through ongoing attention to the interlocking phases of articulating, implementing, and evaluating. Emphasizing the iterative nature of an activated philosophy, we discuss how to sustain an activated philosophy and the benefits of doing so throughout a career. We identify ways to expand your philosophy to promote broader impact and deeper solidification.

First, we recommend taking a synergistic approach to the faculty role; an activated philosophy integrates teaching, scholarship, and service. Next, we discuss the interactive relationship of this activated approach in fostering a teaching–

learning culture. We provide ways to support such a culture, including faculty development, learning communities, team teaching, writing teams, university committee service, and higher education resources and advocacy organizations. Then, we propose ways for connecting an activated teaching philosophy with structural considerations: university mission, professional standards and competencies, promotion and tenure documentation, and accreditation purposes and institutional assessment.

Finally, we discuss sustaining a teaching philosophy and use our personal reflections to illustrate the value of doing so. Activated philosophies can sustain your teaching and have an exponential impact. We close this book with an invitation for you to activate your philosophy and continue the conversation.

Taking a Synergistic Approach to the Faculty Role

One of the most difficult aspects of the faculty role is balancing the three functions of teaching, research, and service (Austin & Pilat, 1990; Fowler, 2015; Weimer, 2010). An activated philosophy can provide needed balance by integrating these roles in a synergistic fashion, which strengthens each function and makes the role of faculty more coherent, more enjoyable, and more doable. The following three examples from our own experience illustrate this synergistic approach.

In Chapter 4 we discussed how Jay spearheaded a professional licensing preparation initiative in an MSW curriculum. This collaborative teaching–learning initiative was rooted in our philosophy and expressed through concrete, implemented steps (e.g., exams that mirrored the licensing exam format) and evaluation of these steps. Synergistically, we developed several SoTL projects that reported on this initiative (Miller et al., 2015). In a further example of synergy, Jay expanded this commitment to professional licensure preparation in the curriculum into his service role. He was appointed by the governor to serve on the state licensure board. Thus, his teaching philosophy is activated in a manner that synergistically combines teaching, scholarship, and service.

In another example, Erlene was compelled by her teaching philosophy's values to give attention to self-care as a professional practice skill. She initiated a self-care assignment in practice courses, which was refined in her team teaching with Jay. Collaborating with other colleagues over several years, we implemented and evaluated a comprehensive curricular initiative. We documented this initiative in various SoTL products (e.g., Grise-Owens, et al., 2018; Grise-Owens, Miller, Escobar-Ratliff, Addison, Marshall, & Trabue, 2016). Building from this initiative, Erlene, Jay, and another colleague formed a community collaboration with two universities and a multistate organization to design, implement, and evaluate an organizational wellness and self-care initiative. This community service role has been documented in additional SoTL products (Miller, Grise-Owens, Addison, Marshall, Trabue, Escobar-Ratliff, 2016). Synergistically, this service initiative feeds back into the teaching role and generates continued scholarship.

In a third example, Larry has a somewhat distinctive role as a branch campus faculty member. For instance, he has an expanded university service role as a designated adviser for all the social work students at this site, and he is the point person and the representative of the social work program. Thus, activation of his teaching philosophy considers his setting and role. For example, his teaching philosophy emphasis on mentoring has implications for this expanded faculty role. Larry has worked with colleagues at the other university branch sites to build a research agenda on studying the faculty experience at branch campuses (Harper, Owens, Funge, & Sullivan, 2017). Thus, his teaching, service, and scholarship are synergistically mutually informing.

These three examples illustrate how to connect teaching, scholarship, and service with university, community, and professional entities. This synergistic approach is integral to the reactivation of your philosophy; that is, the initial articulation, implementation, and evaluation is expanded for broader application. In the beginning of a career in academia, you may be tempted to focus solely on developing the teaching or research aspect of your teaching philosophy. But, we encourage you to quickly consider ways to combine your teaching, service, and scholarship into a synergistic whole. Although it may seem more complicated at first, you will immediately see the value of this approach. Over time, this synergistic approach to the faculty role streamlines your work, solidifies coherence in your roles, energizes your productivity, and broadens your professional impact. The iterative nature of activating your philosophy becomes a synergistic way of fulfilling the teaching, service, and scholarship required in a faculty role.

Fostering a Teaching–Learning Culture

An activated philosophy promotes effective competence in the individual instructor's classroom. Beyond that individual impact, however, activated philosophies can interact with larger contexts of the program unit, school, university, and broader community. Making these connections can highlight the value your teaching brings to these contexts. These connections serve to solidify your own understanding and approach to teaching-and learning within the broader contexts. Likewise, these connections offer an opportunity to contribute and shape the teaching–learning culture of the academic unit, university, and beyond. By *teaching–learning culture*, we mean an environment wherein teaching–learning is valued, and members of that community consistently engage in deliberative, challenging, and collegial ways to develop excellence in teaching and learning (hooks, 1994; Scariono & Liddicoat, 2009). Such a culture provides avenues for you to be supported and engaged in reactivating your philosophy through iterative articulation, implementation, and evaluation.

The previous examples illustrate taking a synergistic approach to a faculty role and are also examples of supporting a teaching–learning culture. That is, in those examples we took our teaching role beyond our individual classes to the broader program and curricula, professional entities, and university context. In a parallel process, we contributed to fostering a broader teaching–learning culture and supported our own faculty development and well-being.

Growing evidence suggests high levels of stress and occupational burnout in academia (Miller, Grise-Owens, & Shalash, 2018). For instance, Amienne (2017) describes the pervasive and insidious effects of abusers and enablers in academia. Harassment, bullying, and mobbing are commonplace (Dellifraine et al., 2014). Call, Owens, and Vincent's (2013) study of social work academic leadership found "that a significant proportion of [administrators] may be not only ineffective but also unethical in their leadership roles" (p. 608). Weimer (2010) cited Karpiak's survey of faculty, who described the university context as a "cold, isolated, fragmented environment" (p. 179). These problematic circumstances are compounded for females, junior faculty (especially those seeking tenure), and underrepresented (e.g., people of color) faculty groups (Davis, 1985; Miller, Taylor, & Bedeian, 2011; Slišković & Seršić, 2011). Indeed, as Palmer (1998) observed, the academic environment can lead faculty to "lose heart" (p. 17). Weimer concluded that faculty burnout, "an extreme form of tired teaching," (p. 174) is underrecognized and largely unaddressed.

The deleterious effects of neglecting the care of your own well-being, faculty development, and instructional development are myriad (Miller et al., 2018; Fowler, 2015; Palmer, 1998). Weimer (2010) concluded, "The absence or very small presence of instructional development [increases] the risk of tired teaching and burnout." (p. 184). The literature on professional burnout clearly identifies ongoing professional development as a key strategy to prevent and address burnout (Grise-Owens, Miller, & Eaves, 2016; Skovholt & Trotter-Mathison, 2011; Wood & McCarthy, 2002).

Against this backdrop, we emphasize the following: The reactivation of your teaching philosophy is challenging and crucial. It is challenging because, regrettably, the academic environment does not always provide (and may actively discourage) the very reactivation that keeps you viable, effective, and healthy. This backdrop means you must be proactive, strategic, and dedicated to your own revitalization. Intentional and ongoing reactivation of your philosophy is the framework for that revitalization.

Reactivating your philosophy requires commitment to faculty development, which can be supported through a structured mentoring process. Also, many faculty annual reviews include a PDP, and even if your context does not require a PDP, we advise having one. Make these processes meaningful through identifying specific ways to reactivate your philosophy.

You must commit to your own development individually. At the same time, the broader structures play a role; that is, your individual development is not solely dependent on institutional support, but it is certainly desirable and helpful. As part of reactivating your philosophy, we encourage you to seek any resources available in your academic unit or university setting.

Typically, universities have teaching–learning centers or faculty development offices. In smaller universities, their functions may be carried out through committees or even less formal mechanisms. Some universities share these resources online for public access (see Appendix A). Make use of all these resources and contribute to them. As we show later in our stories about sustaining an activated philosophy, institutional resources for faculty development have played a key role in reactivating our philosophy. Likewise, reactivating our philosophy produces contributions to the teaching–learning culture of our academic settings and the broader academia.

Learning communities are an excellent format for focused attention to faculty development while fostering a broader teaching–learning culture (Vescio, Ross, & Adams, 2008). The terms *teaching–learning communities*, *faculty learning communities*, and *professional learning communities* are used somewhat interchangeably. As mentioned in Chapter 3, McCormick and Kennelly (2011) used the term *conversation communities* when reporting on study of groups of faculty who met to work on teaching philosophies. Over several decades, colleagues at Miami University have developed an array of resources and guides for establishing formal learning communities (Cox, 2001, 2016; Cox & Richlin, 2004). For example, Richlin & Cox (2004) provided a useful description of using learning communities to develop SoTL. Their website (www.units.miamioh.edu/flc/index.php) provides detailed information on how to develop a learning community, resources for that development, and so forth. *Learning Communities Journal* provides ongoing information and resources for faculty and student learning communities. Notably, these communities can be face-to-face or virtual (Miller, Bosk, Duron, Finno, & Abner, 2016).

In addition to learning communities, team teaching is an excellent way of fostering a teaching–learning community (Buckley, 2000; Zapf, Jerome, & Williams, 2011). When treated as more than simply sharing the workload, team teaching can be of tremendous benefit in activating your philosophy. Team teaching offers an in vivo opportunity to critique and collaborate. With online advances, team teaching can be done virtually across the world and certainly across disciplines and sites (Bowen, 2012). We have had the opportunity to team teach with various colleagues. Jay and Erlene have team taught on multiple occasions. These experiences have provided a ready venue for brainstorming, testing ideas and strategies, and assessing, thus leading to continual refinement of teaching philosophies and SoTL ideas.

Similarly, writing teams (especially with a SoTL focus) are another way to promote a teaching–learning culture (Alexander, Plummer, & McLeod, 2018; Hofek et al., 2010). These writing teams can be in an academic unit, across disciplines, across institutions, and even in global contexts. For example, Marquis, Healey, and Vine (2014) evaluated an international writing team's initiative that was part of the International Society for the Scholarship of Teaching and Learning and identified several benefits of writing groups, including mentoring and leadership, creation of community, diversity of perspectives, experiential learning, and professional development.

These team approaches promote shared collaboration and common norms along with diverse perspectives, all of which are necessary for an effective teaching–learning culture. These team approaches serve to refine and reinforce individual teaching philosophies, and they generate more collaborations. For example, our team teaching and writing groups have produced many SoTL projects. For instance, we've developed a scholarship stream around curricular case examples (Grise-Owens, Cambron, & Valade, 2010; Grise-Owens, & Crum, 2012; Grise-Owens, Drury, & Rickman, 2017; Miller et al., 2015, 2017).

Pragmatically, we advise proactively considering the costs and benefits of team endeavors. For example, be clear from the outset about workload and compensation distribution as well as roles and expectations. In our experience, usually the benefits of team approaches outweigh complications. However, we have had negative experiences because of unequal compensation and differing expectations. Intentional attention to these considerations can solidify the benefits and help you avoid regrettable disappointments or surprises.

As we have emphasized throughout the book, participating in the SoTL movement provides you with a community of scholars with a shared commitment. If your academic unit, university, or even broader discipline does not recognize the value or does not provide adequate avenues for SoTL, consider advocating for it. For example, as mentioned earlier, we contributed an invited article on SoTL to the *Journal of Social Work Education.* Then we successfully arranged with the editor of this premier journal to include Scholarship of Teaching–Learning (SoTL) in the keyword choices for submissions. This simple change has significant ramifications for legitimizing SoTL as a normative topic. In turn, this change encourages and enables more faculty to contribute to SoTL. Pragmatically, publications in such types of premier professional journals typically have more credibility for promotion and tenure purposes.

Similarly, if your academic unit or university does not have a mechanism to support discussions with colleagues about SoTL projects, start one. Initiate a faculty book club, invite colleagues to lunch to discuss a particular SoTL resource, or brainstorm ideas in an online chat. (Hint: Start with this book.)

On a broader scale, develop a teaching–learning community group. For instance, midcareer, Erlene initiated a teaching–learning committee in her academic unit. She made the leadership of this committee part of her PDP and linked her individual PDP to the university's strategic plan and the university's faculty development focus. At their first meeting the committee conceptualized its purpose, goals, and structure. Then it met regularly, facilitated discussion on shared readings in the unit, developed curricular initiatives, and coordinated SoTL projects that included faculty, students, and community partners.

Likewise, Erlene collaborated with interdisciplinary colleagues to establish a university-wide planning group for faculty development. This Faculty Development Committee established a quarterly newsletter, monthly brown bag luncheons for topical conversations about teaching–learning, regular book clubs, annual support for faculty to attend SoTL conferences and report back, an annual showcase of faculty and student scholarship and service, and internal grants for faculty development projects. Erlene initiated and facilitated a group called New Educators' Time for Support for new faculty, whose members presented on their work together at a conference (From, Hersh, Kolb, Holland, & Grise-Owens, 2010). Engaging in these roles revitalized Erlene's teaching spirit, and, pragmatically, these kinds of leadership roles contributed to her promotion to full professor.

Jay learned the importance of participating in these types of peer learning and scholarship networks early in his career. As a doctoral student, he had the opportunity to take part in a national fellowship program centered on child maltreatment prevention work. Participation in this network not only provided Jay with the opportunity to access mentorship networks but also receive feedback on scholarly work approaches from like-minded peers in similar professional circumstances (Miller, Bosk, et al., 2016). Moreover, many of the peer connections that he made have endured, and he continues to collaborate with colleagues on several research projects.

Ideally, these avenues will engender a shared teaching–learning philosophy in academic units or even across university settings. But that level of engagement will vary widely. Again, if your academic unit is not conducive to a teaching–learning culture, take the leadership to encourage that culture. If the resistance or disinterest in the unit is overwhelming, find colleagues in other units of the university (through the avenues mentioned earlier or informally). Regrettably, that kind of resistance or disinterest may be an indicator of poor goodness of fit. Regardless, know that you can find wonderful colleagues by actively engaging with SoTL in conferences, scholarship, online communities and blogs, and other networks.

New faculty are cautioned about taking on too many university service roles, such as serving on committees. In particular, female faculty and faculty of color are tenured at lower rates than Whites and males; excess service obligations are frequently considered to be one of the factors in this inequity (Misra, Lindquist, Holmes, & Agiomavritis, 2011; Reid, 2012). We echo that caution. At the same time, we encourage you to view your service on faculty and university committees as another way to foster a teaching–learning culture (Levine, 2014). In addition to faculty development committees discussed earlier, consider serving on committees such as promotion and tenure and the Faculty Senate. Although often avoided as extra work, these committees have a significant impact on the university culture. Consider using your teaching philosophy as a way of informing the work of these committees. For instance, as part of the university Promotion and Tenure Committee, Erlene served on a subcommittee that revised the promotion and tenure standards. With credible evidence of best practices, she advocated for inclusion of SoTL as part of the standards. Similarly, as mentioned earlier, her collaborative work on the Faculty Development Committee supported significant aspects of the teaching–learning culture.

Finally, we want to advise you of resources, such as the newsletters from your discipline that cover pertinent topics about teaching and learning and higher education. On a broad scale, we recommend the *Chronicle of Higher Education* (https://www.chronicle.com/), a newspaper and website that provides articles, updates, and job listings for faculty. Also, the American Association of University Professors (AAUP; https//www.aaup.com) is an organization that functions to advocate for academic and professional standards and values, such as academic freedom. AAUP's magazine, *Academe*, has timely updates and critical coverage of matters affecting faculty and higher education. Their briefs on these matters help you remain current and at times can ameliorate some of the isolation endemic to academia. That is, you will see that the concerns you have at a local level may be happening on a larger scale or in other locations. The AAUP provides consultation and advocacy for faculty on issues of academic freedom, ethical concerns, and so forth. Over the course of your career, in activating a philosophy, you will benefit from these resources.

We encourage you to proactively connect with these avenues for building a teaching–learning culture, from a local to a global scale. Throughout your career, you will find ideas, strategies, and camaraderie for addressing obstacles and generating improvements in your teaching and higher education. Notably, these connections are even more crucial as more faculty are in off-site, online teaching roles, which can engender isolation and fragmentation.

Activating your philosophy is an individual commitment supported and sustained through connections with others in an intentionally developed, broad-based teaching–learning network. Be intentional and persistent about fostering a teaching–learning community.

Connecting With Structural Considerations

Just as an activated teaching philosophy can expand into broader contexts, it can also have exponential influence through structural considerations. In a mutually beneficial manner, this connection to broader structural considerations helps to reinforce and validate your teaching philosophy.

For instance, as illustrated by Erlene's philosophy statement (see Appendix B), linking your philosophy with the university or program mission reinforces the integral connections and congruence between them. Conversely, it can point out dissonance, which may help identify a poor goodness of fit. Erlene's philosophy statement shows the linkage in one university where she was employed long term. However, you can also use this approach in the job search process. For instance, in presentations for prospective positions, Erlene linked the components of her teaching philosophy with the mission statement of that particular program. Erlene's example can be readily adopted for your philosophy and chosen setting. This linkage can convey congruence and compatibility as well as assess for goodness of fit.

Likewise, an activated philosophy can be linked with broader discipline-specific or interdisciplinary standards. Increasingly, in accordance with the Council for Higher Education Accreditation and other entities, academic programs are required to document adherence to educational standards and competency-based outcomes. Building on McClelland's (1973) formative work, Drisko (2014) provides a useful summary of the movement in higher education to a competency-based approach. In this context, explaining a linkage between one's teaching philosophy and the broader aims of that teaching is pertinent.

Larry illustrates how to connect his philosophy with the CSWE's (2015) Educational Policy and Accreditation Standards competencies (see Table 1 in Appendix C). The CSWE accreditation standards guide social work education in the United States. In Table 1, Larry also connects his teaching philosophy with the Interprofessional Educational Collaborative's (2016) core competencies. These two examples of linking are illustrative and can be adapted to your philosophy and context. Links can show how your teaching philosophy contributes to achieving the required competencies or outcomes of your discipline or interdisciplinary context. In a complementary fashion, the linkages show how your activated philosophy is informed by these competencies or outcomes.

Fox (2013) describes the "centrality of ethics as the undergirding of .... teaching processes" (p. 155) and discussed the NASW's (2017) professional code as it relates to teaching. This discipline-specific example can be applied readily to any professional discipline's code. Finally, Fox emphasizes the AAUP's (2014) position statement of ethics as a guide for academia. Connecting to, or at least considering, these educational and professional mandates is another way to strengthen your philosophy.

An activated teaching philosophy helps educators stay grounded in professional standards and evidence-based practice to ensure effective practice in education. Documenting this activation is exceedingly useful in promotion and tenure processes, which usually involve the drudgery of writing another static exercise similar to the teaching philosophy statement but just a lot more pages. However, through taking the approach of an activated philosophy, the promotion and tenure process becomes more professionally viable and more personally meaningful. Through ongoing activation, you articulate, implement, and evaluate. Your dossier or portfolio is generated from the evidence and artifacts (including SoTL products) you collect in an ongoing fashion. The how-to advice in this book on activating your philosophy provides a framework for sustaining your teaching throughout your career. Happily, this framework also serves the pragmatic purpose of building your ongoing documentation for your annual reviews and promotion and tenure documentation.

In an expansive way, an activated philosophy can also provide pragmatic documentation for accreditation purposes and institutional effectiveness efforts. We have explained the connection between an activated philosophy and a teaching–learning culture and, throughout this book, how SoTL products can be generated from activated philosophies. Institutional assessment and accreditation processes for specific academic programs and at the university level require evidence. For instance, Walvoord & Anderson (2010) provide several useful chapters on parlaying individual course assessments for use in institutional assessment efforts.

SoTL products are excellent evidence of teaching and learning. For example, when preparing documents for the reaccreditation of the MSW where she served as director, Erlene infused multiple examples of SoTL products throughout. The scholarship about faculty's attention to the implicit curriculum (Grise-Owens, Eaves, & Miller, 2013; Miller, Eaves, Grise-Owens, 2014), along with the curricular initiatives for writing (Grise-Owens & Crum, 2012; Grise-Owens, Drury, & Rickman, 2017; Miller, et al, in press), licensure preparation (Miller et al., 2015), self-care as a practice skill (Grise-Owens et al., 2018), and others provided credible documentation of outcomes and fulfillment of accreditation standards.

As you activate your teaching philosophy, consider broader structural links. Minimally, you should be intentional about linking your philosophy with your promotion and tenure processes. With a bit of critical reflection, you can readily link your activated teaching philosophy, SoTL products, and broader structural considerations. Certainly, these links are best supported by a teaching–learning culture but can begin with your activated philosophy. By making these connections, you emphasize the applicability of your philosophy beyond your classroom. Likewise, this linkage reinforces the congruence and relevance between your philosophy and broader structures. Across your career, these expansive connections serve to reactivate your philosophy in an ever broadening and deepening way.

Sustaining an Activated Philosophy

A primary purpose of this book is to provide doctoral and junior faculty with a resource to jump-start their careers through knowing how to activate a teaching philosophy, but the book is for seasoned faculty as well. Short-term, the book is a resource for experienced faculty who might need or want to retool their statements for promotion and awards. More so, this book is offered for those who navigate the role of faculty to use over the course of a career. As colleagues on the journey, we hope the framework we offer in this book can be used throughout your career to sustain your spirit, sharpen your craft, and, by extension, strengthen the impact of education.

Ultimately, the key value of an activated philosophy is how you sustain it and how the philosophy sustains you. From the first year to decades beyond, faculty who want to remain relevant, engaged, and effective will benefit from an activated philosophy. The effects of sustaining it can be exponentially positive and productive.

As we clarified earlier, a teaching philosophy statement is merely a product, a limited road map, a static exercise that is too often boxed up and stored away except when job hunting. But an activated teaching philosophy is an organic process that effectively promotes sustained investment, meaning, and development (Beatty et al., 2009a, 2009b; Kearns & Sullivan, 2011; Owens, Miller, & Grise-Owens, 2014). In some ways, this activation becomes even more crucial after the newness and initial excitement of the faculty role has waned.

Frankly, sustaining the hope, joy, and spirit necessary for ongoing effectiveness and engagement in the faculty role is not a natural occurrence (Ada, 2007; Grise-Owens, 2008, 2011; hooks, 2003; Parker, 1998). Weimer (2010) wrote cogently and authentically about the challenges of midcareer and later career faculty. She asserted that sustaining, "instructional vitality doesn't just happen. … The quest to stay alive and engaged instructionally starts early and lasts right up to the end of the career" (p. 173). Further, she aptly summarized several factors that contribute to "tired teaching and burnout" (p. 174). These factors include (a) stress associated with academic positions, such as heavy workload, being undervalued, role ambiguity, and the lack of feedback; (b) unhealthy institutional environments, with characteristics particularly common to academia including isolation, low pay with high demands, poor leadership, professional animosity, and unresolved conflict; and (c) failure to recognize the emotional energy teaching demands, which is exacerbated by the previous factors. Weimer also discussed beliefs about teaching that inhibit growth, such as denigrating the need to continue learning about the craft of teaching and the overemphasis of the delivery of content versus emphasizing learning as the focus. Weimer concluded that addressing these issues takes "purposeful action" (p. 173).

Extrapolating on Weimer's (2010) astute observations, we contend that an activated teaching philosophy is the "purposeful action" (p. 173) necessary. Next, our stories about sustaining provide examples of what we mean. We began discussing the articulation phase of an activated philosophy by emphasizing the importance of reflecting on core values, beliefs, and inductive experiences. Likewise, Weimer underscored the need for explicit, ongoing attention to your beliefs and values because "what faculty believe about teaching affects how they teach" (p. 194). Attention to faculty development is at the core of Weimer's suggestions for purposeful action. As we emphasized, an activated philosophy requires engaging in SoTL (a primary form of professional development) early, and continuously. Using SoTL to synthesize teaching, research, and service can ameliorate some of the factors mentioned here, such as role ambiguity, overload, and lack of feedback.

Regrettably, academic ennui becomes a reality for some senior faculty. We all know a professor who is using the same syllabus and tired lectures from the first few years of teaching and sometimes not bothering to show up for class. In addition to the purposeful actions to reactive a philosophy, Weimer (2010) advised senior faculty to use advocacy, mentoring, and instructional risk taking to avoid this burnout. An activated philosophy may lead to engagement with broader considerations, such as institutional processes. Weimer pointed out that senior faculty are protected by tenure or simple longevity and can "advocate for instructional causes that faculty not tenured, promoted or contractually secure may find more risky" (p. 201). Likewise, she described how senior faculty have a regenerative function in the mentoring role, which tends to rejuvenate them. Similarly, Weimer urged senior faculty to take instructional risks, which prevents stagnation and are excellent possibilities for SoTL projects.

In Chapter 3 we briefly discussed the activation of our philosophies. We end this book with our stories of sustaining and how the reactivation of a philosophy informs, enhances, and sustains. We also elucidate how we proactively and consistently reiterate the phases of articulation, implementation, and evaluation. We hope our brief stories will inform and encourage your own story and path of sustaining a teaching–learning philosophy.

Larry's Story of Sustaining

As I mentioned in how I articulate my philosophy, I came to academia with more than 25 years of social work practice. Like many second-career teachers, my transition began with part-time teaching while in full-time agency practice. Through mentoring, encouragement, and much consideration, I decided to seek a full-time faculty position, which led to my identification as a pracademic (Owens, 2016). As most faculty search committees request a teaching philosophy statement as a part of the application process, when crafting my teaching philosophy statement (see Appendix B), I emphasized my unique background and experience in social work practice in my statement.

My transition to teaching had challenges; however, I was aided by excellent mentoring and support. Reflecting on that transition and my current status as an associate professor with tenure, I note several factors that particularly helped to activate my philosophy, sustain my teaching, and advance my career. I have sustained and reactivated my philosophy by proactively seeking opportunities for professional development, including engaging in activities I have a particular interest or expertise in; being aware of the importance of understanding and embracing the unique qualities I bring to the faculty role; taking a synergistic approach to the faculty role; and seeking a setting that offers goodness of fit.

Before becoming a full-time faculty member, I attended and presented at numerous professional academic conferences. While in social work agency practice, I found value in the interaction and engagement with the social work field through these avenues. I was able to hear about cutting-edge research in my field, be inspired by the advances in our profession, and develop relationships with other professionals across the country. For example, I routinely participated in child welfare conferences and other professional venues. Furthermore, I routinely contributed to the profession through presentations and service, such as serving as a site visitor for a national child welfare accrediting body and serving on many planning groups.

Along with these professional connections, even before taking a faculty role, I connected with social work education's professional organizations. In particular, the

CSWE's Annual Program Meeting and the Social Work Program Directors' Annual Conference gave me the best introduction to the social work academic world. These experiences and others helped me test my interest in academia. As I moved into the faculty role, I continued active participation in these professional conferences and other venues. Likewise, I combined my professional interest in international issues and personal interest in travel by attending and presenting at several international conferences, including the biennial Joint World Congress on Social Work, Education, and Development; the Euro-American Conference on Academic Disciplines and Creativity; and the International Conference on Environmental, Cultural, Economic, and Social Sustainability.

Since being in the full-time faculty role, I've expanded on my engagement with these teaching–learning venues. In particular, I have focused on developing my SoTL networks. For example, I've presented at and attended the International Lilly Conference on College Teaching, the Teaching Professor Conference, the Wakonse Conference on College Teaching, and other international conferences. Similarly, I've taken advantage of international study abroad and learning opportunities offered by my university and other organizations. I've been able to interact with social work professionals from around the globe, including Australia, Belize, Bolivia, Czech Republic, China, and Taiwan.

All these professional development opportunities occurred because I proactively sought and requested support for these activities, which keep me engaged in the profession and energize my passion for social work and teaching. In a synergistic fashion, these activities reactivate my philosophy by generating new ideas and offering avenues for collegial conversations and scholarly contributions.

Second, another factor that helped me be an effective faculty member is claiming my expertise, and the unique talent and knowledge I bring to the role. My philosophy fits with the expectations of the university and of my academic department; it also meets the expectations of the social work profession (see Appendix C). Because of my background, experience, and expertise, I can offer unique contributions to the faculty role, and I've been able to parlay those unique attributes into a well-defined role.

All the activities associated with the faculty role can be made easier when in the context of the expertise you bring to the faculty role. With my strong identification as a pracademic, I've used that identity to provide professional mentoring for students as they prepare for their careers. Further, I activate my teaching philosophy by using my pracademic identity in making courses relevant and applicable for the social work setting.

Also, in a synergistic manner, I have made pracademic an area of SoTL, and it has generated international connections. For example, when I published an article on being a pracademic (Owens, 2016), I was contacted by two other social work faculty members in Australia, and now we are developing a research study on the experience of pracademic faculty members. Knowing and embracing my unique identity and qualities sustains me in the faculty role and has contributed to my teaching, research, and service agenda for the rest of my teaching career.

Much of the first few years of teaching are focused on preparing classes and producing scholarship and research toward applying for tenure. I learned very quickly that in the world of academia, tenure is the Holy Grail. Even amid normative political barriers that came into play in that process, having an engaged and active teaching philosophy helped maximize my productivity through this phase. Likewise, this activated philosophy provided the structure and products needed for a strong portfolio. Even more so, this activated philosophy helped me retain focus on priorities that are meaningful for me in my faculty role.

Finally, in reflecting on factors that sustain me in my faculty role, I realize the importance of goodness of fit. My identification with my university's emphasis on international reach and being located at one of our university's branch campuses led to a solid goodness of fit. Like many entering the academy, I found the faculty role complex and the university culture quite different from what I was accustomed to or expected. Being primarily located at a branch campus further challenged my acclimation. The faculty role can already be isolating. For faculty at branch campuses, it can be even more so. In addition, faculty at branch campuses often also take on somewhat of a de facto director's role. For example, I am responsible for all the student recruitment and advising for social work students at my branch campus.

My pracademic identity created an excellent goodness of fit with the branch campus location and assignment. Whereas others might find this setting overly challenging, I found it to be the ideal fit for me. Characteristics such as my background in leadership and management, dedication to mentoring, seeing the role of education as preparing professionals, and so forth make this position a particularly congruent fit. Further, as noted earlier, I've taken my unique setting and experience at a branch campus into a line of research. In a writing group and teaching–learning community style, the social work faculty at our branch campuses regularly meet to discuss our work, and together we have begun a line of research on the faculty experience at branch campuses (Harper, Owens, Funge, & Sullivan, 2017).

I hope my experience can reinforce for you the importance of self-reflection on who you are and what you want to be in the faculty role. Then look for a university setting that enables and encourages that identity. Be proactive in seeking resources and opportunities. Ensure that you invest in SoTL and teaching–learning connections. This synergistic approach and reflective reactivation of your philosophy can make your faculty experience more productive, more meaningful, and, thus, more sustainable.

Erlene's Story of Sustaining

As a well-seasoned educator, I can attest that an activated teaching philosophy has, again and again, kept me grounded. Undoubtedly, it has been pivotal in helping me retain my joy in my profession. As I stated in Chapter 3, my teaching philosophy has helped me navigate the vicissitudes of academia from early in my career through attaining full professor and beyond. As I worked my way through academia, my teaching philosophy was my touchstone.

Pragmatically, in promotion and tenure processes, my philosophy was the synergistic thread that integrated the documentation required for these processes. Ongoing, intentional attention to the activation of my teaching philosophy kept me energized and revitalized. Consistently, I tested my philosophy through participating in SoTL, a springboard to an ever evolving, stimulating, and rewarding role of professor, in contrast to the regrettably too common disengagement of senior faculty. I am grateful that the globe of an activated philosophy opened an expansive world of ideas, experiences, and connections.

I could give myriad examples of how intentional investment in reactivating my philosophy has renewed my professional spirit, sharpened my professional competence, and expanded my professional commitment. This reactivation has been helpful in ordinary circumstances, such as updating syllabi routinely and constantly learning new teaching strategies. As earlier examples illustrate, I have actively engaged in faculty development, teaching–learning communities, mentoring, team teaching, and SoTL collaborations and contributions. An activated teaching philosophy has also been particularly valuable in the context of significant changes.

One example was when I was serving as the program director for our graduate program. The university directed our program to adopt a hybrid format (i.e., a balance of course offerings online along with traditional classroom instruction). We were given an expedited time frame to develop a proposal for that change. My teaching philosophy informed my responsibility as the program director to lead these changes and my responsibility as a faculty member to adapt to the hybrid format. My teaching philosophy values empowering, engaging, energizing, encompassing, and evolving processes. For instance, as program director, I practiced these values by seeking initial input, ongoing feedback, and formal evaluation from the students, alumni, and faculty as co-constructors of the new format. Actually, the two student-elected representatives, another faculty member and I, co-presented on the evolution of the hybrid format (Grise-Owens, Escobar-Ratliff, Muse, & Hoffman, 2014). In terms of my teaching role, adapting to the hybrid format illustrates the necessity of having a philosophy that is not bound by a particular modality. For instance, the *E* values of my philosophy are implemented in my commitment to engaging students as co-learners in the process. This commitment is readily translated in an online context to the necessity of ensuring social presence.

In another example, more than a decade ago I was compelled by my evolving teaching philosophy to give explicit attention to preparing graduates in an encompassing way with the self-care skills to avoid burnout in the profession. This commitment stemmed from engaging in interchanges with students and alumni about their experiences of being overwhelmed by stress, seeing the opportunity and responsibility to provide empowering skills to address these concerns, and thus energizing students to enter the profession better prepared to sustain themselves. As mentioned earlier, a cadre of colleagues implemented and assessed a curricular initiative. Self-care as professional practice became a focused area of scholarship for me, which was strengthened by the writing groups and team teaching with colleagues. Likewise, my philosophy's original articulation was expanded through connecting with other streams of holistic pedagogical approaches that mirror the progression of my philosophy's activation (Pyles & Adam, 2016; Witkin, 2014).

Frankly, this pedagogical attention to helping students learn how to prevent burnout was a parallel process for my own journey in the profession. I am not being hyperbolic to assert that a grounded philosophy was pivotal in keeping me centered as I was ejected from a long-term faculty position. As I stated in Chapter 3, my philosophy was explicitly connected with the university's mission statement; this congruence between my philosophy and the university mission statement had attracted me to the university initially. The mission's congruence with my philosophy was a significant determinant of goodness of fit as I taught there for almost two decades.

However, with problematic leadership shifts and other corrosive changes, an incongruence between the university's stated mission and the growing toxicity of the university culture became increasingly difficult to navigate. On November 11, 2016, I was fired from a full, tenured position. Reiterating the details of this firing are not pertinent to this book. Ironically, I was following the guidelines of Weimer's (2010) advice for senior faculty to advocate, mentor, and take risks. The AAUP's (2017) investigative report provides full details, which culminated in the university being censured.

During this challenging time, my activated philosophy remained a touchstone and guide. Throughout the circumstances before, during, and after that firing, I operated as a teacher. With the mentoring function in mind, I sought to model and mirror for students (and alumni) the professional values that underpin my teaching philosophy.

I choose to be transparent about this difficult phase of my career because, regrettably, too many in academia experience similar challenges. Whilst you may not be fired, if you are pursuing your passion and principles of your philosophy, you will experience challenges. That was certainly the case for me and many colleagues. Yet, because of reactivation over time, I have a solidified, synergistic teaching philosophy that frames my professional purpose beyond a particular position.

When I was fired, concerned loved ones and colleagues asked, "Are you going to say you retired?" I replied, "No! That would be a lie. I am not retired. I am *refired*!" At this point in my career, I am not in a faculty position, so I am not teaching in the traditional sense. I am focusing on consultation, training, and scholarship. In actuality, these roles constitute the synergistic facets of a faculty role of service, teaching, and scholarship. Thus, my activated philosophy remains a viable framework. In my current professional work, I continue to practice an empowering, engaging, energizing, encompassing, and evolving philosophy. My reactivated philosophy contributes to sustaining and, indeed, refiring my professional purpose and passion. Authentically, I hope my refirement experience can encourage anyone who may navigate similar challenges on the path.

Jay's Story of Sustaining

So, what does it mean to sustain? Perhaps more pertinently, how do we decide what exactly it is we want to sustain? A few meanings of sustain as a verb are to maintain; keep in existence; keep going; to prolong. Indeed, my actualized philosophy provides a level of sustenance that helps to sustain my professional career as an educator. Likewise, this sustenance provides fodder to continue to sustain and reactivate my philosophy time and again.

First, I want to briefly describe how my philosophy sustains me. As I said in my Articulation segment in Chapter 3, identity is important, and mine, like others, is complex. If I may be candid (and a bit vulnerable), as a millennial faculty member of color I sometimes experience the navigation of academe as cumbersome and complex. To get a better sense of these complexities, one need look no further than the reams of academic literature and research documenting these challenges (Alexander & Moore, 2008; Johnson-Bailey & Cervero, 2008; Turner, Gonzalez, & Wood, 2008). I find my actualized philosophy to be a valuable tool in traversing some of these complexities.

My activated philosophy is my proverbial beacon. Beacons are often used as navigational tools to guide people to a certain place. My philosophy guides my teaching. It lets me know where I have been and where I am going. Perhaps most important, it offers insight into where I may go. In this way, my philosophy sustains me.

Now, a tad about how I sustain my philosophy. Simply put, I sustain my philosophy through my fervent desire to be the best educator I can be. Given my personal experiences (e.g., having been in out of home care), I know the impact that my students may have when they leave my course. Education is not just about tests, essays, and grades. Many of my students will go on to intervene in someone's life, perhaps at the person's time of most need. Because of my practice experiences, I know the challenges they may face in doing so.

I expect my students to give their best, and to do so knowing they have the requisite training and education to deal with complex practice scenarios. Likewise, I expect from myself that I will do my best ensuring they have the best educational experience possible. An actualized, sustained philosophy is a primary way to achieve this aim.

As discussed earlier, my experiences with mentoring and team teaching have supported my growth as a faculty member. Also, I have found engagement in SoTL paramount to sustaining my philosophy. Beginning as a graduate student, I made presentations at conferences with my mentor and other colleagues. Over the years I have had many opportunities to present works related to my teaching philosophy in national and international venues. I have also been fortunate enough to publish several papers about teaching and learning, particularly in the context of social work education. Engagement in these types of activities have always been refreshing, and interacting with this network of colleagues has been helpful in normalizing some of the challenges I face in teaching and learning.

Of course some very pragmatic elements make sustaining my philosophy necessary. Currently, I am a nontenured, junior-level (i.e., assistant professor) faculty member. Working toward tenure certainly serves as a motivation (though not my primary motivation) to sustaining and living an actualized philosophy.

With this backdrop, as a social work educator I engage fully in the three aspects of that role: research and scholarship, teaching, and service (Boyer, 1990). Being mindful of these roles, and the intentionality of ensuring consistency among them, serves as a mechanism for sustaining my philosophy. I am dedicated to service endeavors that complement my teaching, and likewise, my teaching and service endeavors inform my research. This congruency informs, and subsequently helps me to sustain, my philosophy.

Earlier I posed a question: How do we decide what exactly it is we want to sustain? For me, it is simple: I engage in the framework described in this book. Being deliberate about all phases of actualizing my philosophy—articulation, implementation, evaluation, and reactivation—helps me grapple with this query effectively. Through the reactivation process, I decide what I want to sustain.

I sincerely hope the process detailed in this book does for you what it did and continues to do for me: helps identify what it is that sustains you as an educator. Further, I hope you finish the book with more questions than answers because it is through exploring these queries that you sharpen your ideas about teaching and learning and, ultimately, live your actualized philosophy.

An Activated Teaching–learning Philosophy: A Globe, Not Just a Road Map

Faculty interested in consistent integrity and constant renewal will find the articulation, implementation, and evaluation of their philosophy meaningful and essential. This book provides specific elements, pragmatic steps, suggested resources, and illustrative examples for you to use in activating a teaching–learning philosophy. This foundational and flexible framework can be adapted to develop your own distinctive and viable philosophy.

As we have emphasized, essentially a teaching philosophy statement is a road map for a one-time purpose: to get from Point A (job interview) to Point B (get a job). In contrast, an activated philosophy is akin to a globe; an activated philosophy expands your worldview. A teaching philosophy statement, without activation, is a static product. If you do not go beyond this initial road map, you risk being stuck on the same road. Although initially interesting, over time this road becomes rutted by routine. But if you decide to activate a philosophy, it will expand your horizons. Exploring this globe through purposeful actions, you will have interesting, challenging, meaningful, and adventurous treks. You will discover and contribute to developing a diverse and delightful terrain of teaching and learning. You will become a more adept traveler teacher and a more engaged learner. This expansive worldview, your activated teaching philosophy, will sustain your teaching spirit and generate transformative learning experiences.

We close with an invitation: Take purposeful action. Articulate, implement, evaluate, and reactivate your philosophy. We hope this book serves as a trusty companion as you traverse this demanding, meaningful, and important journey as an educator. We hope our collegial examples inspire you to share your activated philosophy through SoTL contributions. We look forward to continued conversation as our paths intersect across the globe, either directly or through the teaching commons of SoTL. Activate on!

References

Ada, A. F. (2007). A lifetime of learning to teach. *Journal of Latinos and Education, 6*, 103–118.

Adams, M., Bell, L. A., & Griffin, P. (2007). *Teaching for diversity and social justice* (5th ed.). New York, NY: Routledge.

Agrawal, S., Szatmari, P., & Hanson, M. (2008). Teaching evidence-based psychiatry: Integrating and aligning the formal and hidden curricula. *Academic Psychiatry, 32*, 470–474.

Albers, C. (2003). Using the syllabus to document the scholarship of teaching. *Teaching Sociology, 31*(1), 60–72.

Alexander, F. K. (2000). The changing face of accountability: Monitoring and assessing institutional performance in higher education. *Journal of Higher Education, 71*, 411–431.

Alexander, P., Chabot, K., Cox, M., DeVoss, D. N., Gerber, B., Perryman-Clark, S., … Wendt, M. (2012). Teaching with technology: Remediating the teaching philosophy statement. *Computers and Composition, 29*(1), 23–38.

Alexander, R., & Moore, S. E. (2008). The benefits, challenges, and strategies of African American faculty teaching at predominantly White institutions. *Journal of African American Studies, 12*, 4–18.

Alexander, J., Plummer, L., & McLeod, J. (2018, May-June). Addressing gendered practices through women's writing groups, *Academe*, 23–26.

American Association for Higher Education. (1991). *Nine principles of good practice for assessing student learning*. Sterling, VA: Stylus.

American Association of University Professors. (2014). *Policy documents and reports*. Baltimore, MD: Johns Hopkins University Press.

American Association of University Professors. (2017). Academic freedom and tenure: Spalding University (Kentucky). *Academe, 103*(5), 12–24.

Amienne, K. K. (2017, November 2). Abusers and enablers in faculty culture. *Chronicle of Higher Education*. Retrieved from https://www.chronicle.com/article/AbusersEnablersin/241648

Anastas, J. W. (2010). *Teaching in social work: An educators' guide to theory and practice*. New York, NY: Columbia University Press.

Angelo, T. A., & Cross, K. P. (1993). *Classroom assessment techniques: A handbook for college teachers*. San Francisco, CA: Jossey-Bass.

Aruguete, M. S., Slater, J., & Mwaikinda, S. R. (2017). The effects of professors' race and clothing style on student evaluations. *Journal of Negro Education, 86*, 494–502.

Askeland, G., & Payne, M. (2006). The post-modern student: Piloting through uncertainty. *Journal of Teaching in Social Work, 24*, 167–179.

Austin, A. E., & Pilat, M. (1990). Tension, stress, and the tapestry of faculty lives. *Academe, 76*(1), 38-42.

Bain, K. (2004). *What the best college teachers do*. Cambridge, MA: Harvard University Press.

Balmer, D. G., Master, C. L., Richards, B., & Giardino, A. P. (2009). Implicit versus explicit curricula in general pediatrics education: Is there a convergence? *Pediatrics, 124*, e347–e354.

Baker, A. C., Jensen, P. J., & Kolb, D. A. (2002). *Conversational learning: An experiential approach to knowledge creation*. Westport, CT: Quorum Books.

Barker, R. (2003). *The social work dictionary*. (5th ed.). Washington, DC: NASW Press.

Bandura, A. (1977). Self-efficacy: Toward a unifying theory of behavioral change. *Psychological Review, 84*, 191–215.

Barber, B. R. (2007). *Consumed—How markets corrupt children, infantilize adults, and swallow citizens whole*. New York, NY: Norton.

Bean, J. C. (2001). *Engaging ideas: The professor's guide to integrating writing, critical thinking, and active learning in the classroom*. San Francisco, CA: Jossey-Bass.

Beatty, J. E., Leigh, J. S. A, & Dean, K. L. (2009a). Finding our roots: An exercise for creating a personal teaching philosophy statement. *Journal of Management Education, 33*(1), 115–130.

Beatty, J. E., Leigh, J. S. A, & Dean, K. L. (2009b). Philosophy rediscovered: Exploring the connections between teaching philosophies, educational philosophies, and philosophy. *Journal of Management Education, 33*(1), 99–114.

Belenky, M. F., Clinchy, B. M., Goldberger, N. R., & Tarule, J. M. (1997). *Women's way of knowing: The development of self, voice, and mind*. New York, NY: Basic Books.

Belenky, M. F., & Stanton, A. V. (2000). Inequality, development and connected knowing. In J. Mezirow and Associates, *Learning as transformation: Critical perspectives on a theory in progress* (pp. 71–102). San Francisco: Jossey-Bass.

Berry, T. (2015). *Take the wheel, steer your business*. Retrieved from https://www.americanexpress.com/us/small-business/openforum/articles/steering-business-steady-course/

Biggs, J. (1999) What the student does: Teaching for enhanced learning. *Higher Education Research & Development, 18*(1), 57–75,

Billings, M. E., Engelbert, R., Curtis, J. R., Block, S., & Sullivan, A. M. (2010). Determinants of medical students' perceived preparation to perform end-of-life care, quality of end-of-life care education, and attitudes toward end-of-life care. *Journal of Palliative Medicine, 13*, 319–326.

Birkenmaier, J., Cruce, A., Burkemper, E., Curley, J., Wilson, R. J., & Stretch, J. J. (Eds.). (2011). *Educating for social justice: Transformative experiential learning.* Chicago, IL: Lyceum Books.

Bishop-Clark, C., & Dietz-Uhler, B. (2012). *Engaging in the scholarship of teaching and learning: A guide to the process, and how to develop a project from start to finish.* Sterling, VA: Stylus.

Blankenship, B. T., & Stewart, A. J. (2017). Intersectional identities, identity dimensions, and academic contingencies of self-worth. *Identity, 17*, 109–124.

Bloom, B., Englehart, M. Furst, E., Hill, W., & Krathwohl, D. (1956). *Taxonomy of educational objectives: The classification of educational goals. Handbook I: Cognitive domain.* New York, NY: Longmans, Green.

Bogo, M., & Wayne, J. (2013). The implicit curriculum in social work education: The culture of human interchange. *Journal of Teaching in Social Work, 31*, 2–14.

Boring, A. (2017). Gender biases in student evaluations of teaching. *Journal of Public Economics, 145*, 27–41.

Borton, T. (1970). *Reach, touch, and teach: Student concerns and process education.* New York, NY: McGraw-Hill.

Bowen, J. A. (2012). *Teaching naked: How moving technology out of your college classroom will improve student learning.* San Francisco, CA: Jossey-Bass.

Boyer, E. L. (1990). *Scholarship reconsidered: Priorities of the professoriate.* Princeton, NJ: Carnegie Foundation for the Advancement of Teaching.

Boysen, G. A. (2012). Teacher and student perceptions of microaggressions in college classrooms. *Journal of College Teaching, 60*, 122–129.

Brilliant, E. (1986). Social work leadership: A missing ingredient? *Social Work, 31*, 325–331.

Brookfield, J. (1995). *Becoming a critically reflective teacher.* San Francisco, CA: Basic Books.

Brookfield, S. D. (2015). The *skillful teacher: On technique, trust, and responsiveness in the classroom* (3rd ed.). San Francisco, CA: Jossey-Bass.

Brown, S. B., Collard, R., & Hoogeveen, D. (2014). Pedagogical declarations: Feminist engagements with the teaching statement. *Journal of Geography in Higher Education, 38*(1), 148–154.

Buckley, F. J. (2000). *Team teaching: What, why, how.* Thousand Oaks, CA: SAGE.

Bulik, R. & Shokar, G. (2007). "Coming about!"—a faculty workshop on teaching beliefs. *Teaching and Learning in Medicine, 19*, 168–173.

Burghardt, S. (2013). *Macro practice in social work for the 21st century: Bridging the macro-micro divide.* (2nd ed.) Thousand Oaks, CA: SAGE

Buskist, W., & Davis, S. F. (Eds.). (2006). *Handbook of the teaching of psychology.* Boston, MA: Blackwell.

Call, C., Owens, L. W., & Vincent, N. J. (2013). Leadership in social work education: Sustaining collaboration and mission. *Advances in Social Work, 14,* 594–612.

Caughie, P. (2007). Impassioned teaching. *Academe, 93*(4), 54–55.

Caughlin, D. E. (2014). Enhancing your teaching experience: Developing your teaching philosophy, course syllabus, and teaching portfolio. *Industrial-Organizational Psychologist, 52*(2), 94–99.

Caulfield, J. (2011). *How to design and teach a hybrid course: Achieving student-centered learning through blended classroom, online, and experiential activities.* Sterling, VA: Stylus.

Chang, H., & Boyd, D. (Eds.). (2011). *Spiritually in higher education.* Walnut Creek, CA: Left Coast Press.

Chism, N. V. N. (1998). Developing a philosophy of teaching statement. *Essays on Teaching Excellence, 9*(3), 1–2.

Christiansen, M. (2016). A deliberate pedagogy—Introducing the hidden curriculum, social pedagogy, and the common third. In L. Pyles & G. J. Adam (Eds.), *Holistic engagement: Transformative social work education in the 21st century.* (pp. 115–137). New York, NY: University of Oxford Press.

Clark, G. D. (2013, October 29). Beyond the teaching statement. *Chronicle of Higher Education.* Retrieved from https://www.chronicle.com/blogs/onhiring/beyond-the-teaching-statement/41019.

Clouder, L. (2000). Reflective practice: Realising its potential. *Physiotherapy, 86,* 517–522.

Collins, J. (2001). *Good to great: Why some companies make the leap ... and others don't.* New York, NY: HarperCollins.

Collins, J., & Pratt, D. (2011). The Teaching Perspectives Inventory at 10 years and 100,00 respondents: Reliability and validity of a teacher self-report inventory. *Adult Education Quarterly, 61,* 358–375.

Coppola, B. P. (2002). Writing a statement of teaching philosophy: Fashioning a framework for your classroom. *Journal of College Science Teaching, 31,* 448–453.

Council on Social Work Education. (2015). *Educational policy and accreditation standards.* Retrieved from https://www.cswe.org/Accreditation/Standards-and-Policies/2015-EPAS

Cox, M. D. (2001). Faculty learning communities: Change agents for transforming institutions into learning organizations. *To Improve the Academy, 19*(1), 69–93.

Cox, M. D. (2016). Achievement of faculty learning community extremes:

Impossible, modified and hybrid FLCs, and the "belonging" outcome. *Learning Communities Journal, 8*(1), 1–7.

Cox, M. D., & Richlin, L. (2004). Building faculty learning communities [Special issue]. *New Directions for Teaching and Learning*, 97.

Creasey, G., Jarvis, P., and Knapcik, E. (2009). A measure to assess student-instructor relationships. *International Journal for the Scholarship of Teaching and Learning, 3*(2), 1–10.

Crookes, G. (2009). *Values, philosophies, and beliefs in TESOL: Making a statement.* New York, NY: Cambridge University Press.

Cullen, C. (2013). Making syllabus more than contract. In M. Weimer (Ed.), *Teaching strategies for the college classroom: A collection of faculty articles* (pp. 22–24). Madison, WI: Magna.

Dahlgren, L. O., Eriksson, B. E., Gyllenhammar, H., Korkeila, M., & Saaf-Rothoff, A. (2006). To be and to have a critical friend in medical teaching. *Journal of Medical Education, 40*(1), 5–6.

Davis, L. E. (1985). Black and White social work faculty: Perceptions of respect, satisfaction, and job permanency. *Journal of Sociology & Social Welfare, 12*, 79–85.

Dean, R. G. (2007). "Good talk": The art of transforming conversations. In S. L. Witkin, & D. Saleebey, *Social work dialogues: Transforming the canon in inquiry, practice, and education* (pp. 38–63). Alexandria, VA: Council on Social Work Education.

DelliFraine, J. L., McClelland, L. E., Erwin, C. O., & Wang, Z. (2014). Bullying in academia: Results of a survey of health administration faculty. *Journal of Health Administration Education, 31*(2), 147–163.

Dewey, J. (1910). *How we think.* Boston, MA: D. C. Heath.

Dewey, J. (1934). *Art as experience.* New York, NY: Perigee.

Dewey, J. (1938) *Experience and education.* New York, NY: Macmillan.

Driscoll, M. P. (2004). *Psychology of learning for instruction* (3rd ed.). Needham Heights, MA: Allyn & Bacon.

Drisko, J. W. (2014). Competencies and their assessment. *Journal of Social Work Education, 50*, 414–426.

Drolet, J. (2013). Statement of teaching philosophy: My role as field education coordinator. *Social Work Education, 32*, 274–277.

DuBois, B. L., & Miley, K. K. (2011). *Social work: An empowering profession* (7th ed.). Boston, MA: Pierson.

Duquesne University. (n.d.). *Statement of teaching philosophy.* Retrieved from https://www.duq.edu/about/centers-and-institutes/center-for-teaching-excellence/academic-careers/landing-an-academic-job/statement-of-teaching-philosophy.

Eisner, E. W. (2002). *The arts and the creation of mind.* New Haven, CT: Yale University Press.

Eierman, R. J. (2008). The teaching philosophy statement: Purposes and organizational structure. *Journal of Chemical Education, 85*, 336–338.

Ellis, D. & Griffin, G. (2000). Developing a teaching philosophy statement: A special challenge for graduate students. *Journal of Graduate Teaching Assistant Development, 7*(2), 85–92.

Ertmer, P. A., & Newby, T. J. (1993). Behaviorism, cognitivism, constructivism: Comparing critical features from an instructional design perspective. *Performance Improvement Quarterly, 6*(4), 50–72

Execution. (n.d.) In *Merriam-Webster's online dictionary* (11th ed.). Retrieved from https://www.merriam-webster.com/dictionary/execution

Felicilda-Reynaldo, R. F. D., & Utley, R. (2015). Reflections of evidence-base practice in nurse educators' teaching philosophy statements. *Nurse Education Perspectives, 36*(2). 89—95.

Figueira-McDonough, J., Netting, F. E., & Nichols-Casebolt, A. (Eds.). (1998). *The role of gender in practice knowledge: Claiming half the human experience*. New York, NY: Garland.

Fink, L. D. (2003) *Creating significant learning experiences: An integrated approach to designing college courses*. San Francisco, CA: Jossey-Bass.

Fitzmaurice, M. (2008). Voices from within: Teaching in higher education as a moral practice. *Teaching in Higher Education, 13*, 341–352.

Flaherty, C. (May 22, 2018). Teaching eval shake-up. *Inside Higher Ed*. Retrieved from https://www.insidehighered.com/news/2018/05/22/most-institutions-say-they-value-teaching-how-they-assess-it-tells-different-story

Fook, J., & Askeland, A. (2007). Challenges of critical reflections: "Nothing ventured, nothing gained." *Social Work Education, 26*, 520–533.

Fowler, S. (2015). Burnout and depression in academia: A look at the discourse of the university. *Empedocles: European Journal for the Philosophy of Communication, 6*, 155–167.

Fox, R. (2011). *The use of self: The essence of professional education*. Chicago, IL: Lyceum Books.

Fox, R. (2013). *The call to teach: Philosophy, process, and pragmatics of social work education*. Alexandria, VA: CSWE Press.

Freire, P. (1998a). *Pedagogy of freedom: Ethics, democracy, and civic courage*. NY: Rowman & Littlefield.

Freire, P. (1998b). *Teachers as cultural workers: Letters to those who dare teach*. Boulder, CO: Westview Press.

Freire, P. (2007a). *Education for critical consciousness*. New York, NY: Continuum.

Freire, P. (2007b). *Pedagogy of the oppressed*. New York, NY: Continuum.

From, A., Hersh, K., Kolb, C, Holland, L, & Grise-Owens, E. (November 19, 2010). *New Educators' Time for Support (NETS): Impact of a learning community for new faculty*. Paper presented at the Lilly International Conference on College Teaching, Miami University, Oxford, OH.

Gagne, R. (1962). Military training and principles of learning. *American Psychologist, 17*, 263–276.

Gagne, R. (1985). *The conditions of learning* (4th ed.). New York, NY: Holt, Rinehart & Winston.

Gagne, R. (1987). *Instructional technology foundations*. Hillsdale, NJ: Erlbaum.

Gagne, R., Briggs, L., & Wager, W. (1992). *Principles of instructional design* (4th ed.). Fort Worth, TX: HBJ College Publishers.

Gagne, R. & Driscoll, M. (1988). *Essentials of learning for instruction* (2nd ed.). Englewood Cliffs, NJ: Prentice-Hall.

Gardner, H. (2011). *Frames of mind: The theory of multiple intelligences*. New York, NY: Basic Books.

Germain, C. B. (1991) *Human behavior in the social environment: An ecological view.* New York, NY: Columbia University Press.

Gibbs, G., Knapper, C., & Picinnin, S. (2007). The role of departmental leadership in fostering excellent teaching. *Engage11*. London, UK: Leadership Foundation.

Giroux, H. (1988). *Teachers as intellectuals: Toward a critical pedagogy of learning.* Wesport, CT: Bergin & Garvey.

Glaser, M. (2008). A brief statement of my teaching philosophy. *Faculty Focus*, Retrieved from https://www.facultyfocus.com/articles/a-brief-statement-of-my-philosophy-of-teaching/

Gofton, W., & Regehr, G. (2006). What we don't know we are teaching: Unveiling the hidden curriculum. *Clinical Orthopedics and Related Research, 449*, 20–27.

Goldberger, N., Tarule, J., Clinchy, B., & Belenky, M. (Eds.). (1996). *Knowledge, difference, and power: Essays inspired by* Women's Way of Knowing. New York, NY: Basic Books.

Goldstein, H. (2001*). Experiential learning: A foundation for social work education and practice.* Alexandria, VA: Council on Social Work Education.

Goodyear, G. E., & Allchin, D. (1998). Statements of teaching philosophy. In M. Kaplan & D. Lieberman (Eds.), *To improve the academy: Resources for faculty, instructional, and organizational development* (Vol. 17, pp. 103–122). Stillwater, OK: New Forums Press.

Gottfried, P. (2002). About consumerist education. *Academic Questions*, 15(2), 53–58.

Graham, M. A. (1997). Empowering social work faculty. *Journal of Teaching in Social Work, 15*(1/2), 33–49.

Grise-Owens, E. (2002). Sexism in the social work curriculum: A content analysis of the *Journal of Social Work Education, 1998–99. Affilia, 17*, 147–166.

Grise-Owens, E. (2008). Killing canaries: A bird's eye view. *Reflections: Narratives from Helping Professions, 14*(1), 31–38.

Grise-Owens, E. (2011). Pedagogy and spirituality in higher education: Perspectives, practices, and possibilities. In H. Chang & D. Boyd (Eds.) *Spirituality in higher education: Autoethnographies* (pp. 147–162). Walnut Creek, CA: Left Coast Press.

Grise-Owens, E., Cambron, S., & Valade, R. (2010). Using current events to enhance learning experiences: A social work curricular case example. *Journal of Social Work Education, 46*, 133–146.

Grise-Owens, E., & Crum, K. (2012). Teaching writing as a professional practice skill: A social work curricular case example. *Journal of Social Work Education, 48*, 517–536.

Grise-Owens, E., Drury, W., & Rickman, C. (2017, March). *Using a holistic view of competence to develop a professional writing course.* Paper presented at the Association of Baccalaureate Social Work Program Directors conference, New Orleans, LA.

Grise-Owens, E., Eaves, M., & Miller, J. (2013, November). *Conceptualizing and evaluating implicit curriculum: Accessing student voice through autoethnography.* Paper presented at the Annual Program Meeting of the Council on Social Work Education, Dallas, TX.

Grise-Owens, E., Escobar-Ratliff, L., Muse, M., & Hoffman, K. (2014, April). "Enchiladas and on-line teaching–learning: A menu for success." Workshop conducted at a meeting of Kentucky Association of Social Work Educators, Bowling Green, KY.

Grise-Owens, E., & Jones, A. (2014, March). *Using an integrated assignment to promote professionalism in and beyond the classroom.* Paper presented at the annual conference of the Association of Baccalaureate Social Work Program Directors, Louisville, KY.

Grise-Owens, E., & Lay, K. (Eds.). (2009). Inside out: Reflections on personal and professional intersections [Special issue]. *Reflections—Narratives of Professional Helping, 15*(2).

Grise-Owens, E., Miller, J., & Eaves, M. (2016). *The A-to-Z self-care handbook for social workers and other helping professionals.* Harrisburg, PA: New Social Worker Press.

Grise-Owens, E., Miller, J., Escobar-Ratliff, L., Addison, D., Marshall, M., & Trabue, D. (2016). A field practicum experience in designing and developing a wellness initiative: An agency and university partnership. *Field Educator, 6*(2), 1–19.

Grise-Owens, E., Miller, J., Escobar-Ratliff, L., & George, N. (2018). Teaching Note—Teaching self-care and wellness as a professional practice skill: A curricular case example. *Journal of Social Work Education, 54*, 180–186.

Grise-Owens, E., Miller, J., & Owens, L. W. (2014). Responding to global shifts: "Meta"—Practice as a relevant social work practice paradigm. *Journal of Teaching in Social Work, 34*, 46–59.

Grise-Owens, E., Miller, J., & White, J. (2007, October). *Choppin' it up about liberatory learning: Next generation's pedagogical possibilities*. Paper presented at the Annual Program Meeting of the Council on Social Work Education, San Francisco, CA.

Grise-Owens, E., Owens, L. W., & Miller, J. (2016a). Conceptualizing scholarship of teaching and learning (SoTL) for social work education. *Journal of Social Work Education, 52*, 6–17.

Grise-Owens, E., Owens, L. W., & Miller, J. (2016b). Recasting licensing in social work: "Something more" for professionalism. *Journal of Social Work Education, 52(Suppl.*, 1), S126–S133.

Grise-Owens, E., & Steen, T. (2013, April). *Use of "Indicators of Professionalism" assignment to promote professionalism: Student and faculty perspectives*. Paper presented at the Kentucky Association of Social Work Educators, Asbury, KY.

Grundman, H. G. (2006). Writing a teaching philosophy statement. *Notices of the American Mathematical Society, 53*, 1329–1333.

Gurung, R. A. R., & Schwartz, B. M. (2010). Riding the third wave of SoTL. International *Journal for the Scholarship of Teaching and Learning, 4*(2), 1–6.

Gutiérrez, L. M. (2012). From the editor—Recognizing and valuing our roles as mentors, *Journal of Social Work Education, 48*, 1–4.

Haggerty, K. D. (2010, February 19). Teaching statements are bunk. *Chronicle of Higher Education*. Retrieved from https://www.chronicle.com/article/Teaching-Statements-Are-Bunk/64152

Harper, W., Owens, L. W., Funge, S. P., & Sullivan, D. J. (2017). Teaching at branch campuses: The faculty experience. *Access: The Journal of the National Association of Branch Campus Administrators 3*(1), 1–15.

Harrington, C., & Gabert-Quillen, C. (2015). Syllabus length and use of images: An empirical investigation of student perceptions. *Scholarship of Teaching and Learning in Psychology, 1*, 235–243.

Healey, M. (2003). *The scholarship of teaching and learning in academic careers*. Sterling, VA: Stylus.

Hickson, H. (2011). Critical reflection: Reflecting on learning to be reflective. *Reflective Practice, 12*, 829–839.

Hofek, J. F., Kaiser, K. L., Visovsky, C., Barry, T. L., Nelson, A. E., Kaiser, M. M., & Miller, C. L. (2010). Using a writing group to promote faculty scholarship. *Nurse Educator, 35*(1), 41–45.

Holloway, S., Black, P., Hoffman, K., & Pierce, D. (2008). *Some considerations of the import of the 2008 EPAS for curriculum redesign*. Unpublished white paper.

hooks, b. (1994). *Teaching to transgress: Education as the practice of freedom*. New York, NY: Routledge.

hooks, b. (2003). *Teaching community: A pedagogy of hope*. New York, NY: Routledge.

Huber, M. T. (2010). CASTL has concluded. Long live the scholarship of teaching and learning! *Arts and Humanities in Higher Education, 9*(1), 5–8.

Huber, M. T., & Hutchings, P. (2005). *The advancement of learning: Building the teaching commons.* San Francisco, CA: Jossey-Bass.

Huisman, J., & Currie, J. (2004). Accountability in higher education: Bridge over troubled water? *Higher Education, 48*, 529–551.

Hutchings, P. (2010). The scholarship of teaching and learning: From idea to integration. *New Directions for Teaching and Learning, 123*, 63–72.

Hutchings, P., Huber, M. T., & Ciccone, A. (2011). *The scholarship of teaching and learning reconsidered: Institutional integration and impact.* San Francisco, CA: Jossey-Bass.

Interprofessional Education Collaborative. (2016). *IPEC Core Competencies for Interprofessional Collaboration Practice: 2016 update.* Retrieved from https://www.asha.org/uploadedFiles/Interprofessional-Collaboration-Core-Competency.pdf

Jaspers, K. (1951). *Way to wisdom: An introduction to philosophy.* New Haven, CT: Yale University Press.

Jenkins, J. S., Bugeja, A. D., & Barber, L. K. (2014). More content or more policy? A closer look at syllabus detail, instructor gender, and perceptions of instructor effectiveness. *College Teaching, 62*, 129–135.

Jensen, D. (2017). Mentoring in a distributed learning social work program. *Journal of Social Work Education, 53*, 637–650.

Jennings, T. (2010). Teaching "out" in the university: An investigation into the effects of lesbian, bisexual, and transgender faculty self-disclosure upon student evaluations of faculty teaching effectiveness in the USA. *International Journal of Inclusive Education, 14*, 325–339.

Jensen, J. L., Kummer, T. A., & Godoy, P. D. (2015). Improvements from a flipped classroom may simply be the fruits of active learning. *Cell Biology Education: Life Sciences Education, 14*, 1–12.

Jogerst, M., & Luna Jackson, J. (2017, October). *Teaching statement writing.* Workshop conducted at the Annual Program Meeting of the Council on Social Work Education, Dallas, TX.

Johnson-Bailey, J., & Cervero, R. M. (2008). Different worlds and divergent paths: Academic careers defined by race and gender. *Harvard Educational Review, 78*, 311–429.

Kaplan, M., Meizlish, D., O'Neal, C., & Wright, M.C. (2007). A research-based rubric for developing statements of teaching philosophy. *To Improve the Academy*, 26, 242–262.

Kearns, K. D., & Sullivan, C. S. (2011). Resources and practices to help graduate students and postdoctoral fellows write statements of teaching philosophy. *Advances in Physiology Education, 35*, 136–145.

Keaton, A. F. (2015). Teaching students the importance of professionalism. *Teaching Professor, 29*(6), 5.

Kilmer, J. J. (2007). Reclaim your rights as a liberal educator. *Academe, 93*(4), 56-58.

Knowles, M. S., Holton, E. F., & Swanson, R. A. (2005). *The adult learner: The definitive classic in adult education and human Resource development*. Boston: Taylor & Francis Ltd.

Kogan, L. R., Schoenfeld-Tacher, R., & Hellyer, P. W. (2010). Student evaluations of teaching: Perception of faculty based on gender, position, and rank. *Teaching in Higher Education, 15*, 623–636.

Kolb, D. A. (1981). Learning styles and disciplinary differences. In Chickering, A. W. and Associates (Eds.) *The Modern American College*. San Francisco, Jossey-Bass Publishers. pp. 232-255.

Kolb, D. (1984). *Experiential learning: Experience as the source of learning*. New York, NY: Prentice Hall.

Krathwohl, D. R. (2002). A revision of Bloom's taxonomy: An overview. *Theory into Practice, 41*, 212–218.

Krysik, J. L., & Finn, J. (2013). *Research for effective social work practice* (3rd ed.). New York, NY: Routledge.

Lage, M. J., Platt, G. J., & Treglia, M. (2000). Inverting the classroom: A gateway to creating an inclusive learning environment. *Journal of Economic Education, 31*(1), 30–43.

Laird, D. (1985). *Approaches to Training and Development*. Harlow: Addison Wesley.

Lang, J. M. (2016). *Small teaching: Everyday lessons from the science of learning*. San Francisco, CA: Jossey-Bass.

Lao Tzu (1989). *Tao teh ching* [Translated title]. (J. C. H. Wu, Trans.). Boston, MA: Shambhala.

Lawrence, J.W. (2018, May-June). Student evaluations of teaching are not valid. *Academe, 16-18.*

Lay, K. (2005). Transformative events—transformative stories. *Reflections: Narratives of Professional Helping, 11*(3), 20–26.

Lay, K., & McGuire, L. (2010). Building a lens for critical reflection and reflexivity in social work education. *Social Work Education, 29*, 539–550.

Levine, A. G. (2014). Leveraging committee assignments for advancements. *Science, 343*, 685–688.

Licklider, B. (2004). An eloquent, insightful teaching philosophy. *Teaching Professor, 18*(10), 1.

Light G., & Cox, R. (2001). *Learning and teaching in higher education: The reflective professional.* London, UK: P. Chapman.

Maclean, S. (2010). *The social work pocket guide to ... reflective practice*. Rugeley, UK: Kirwin Maclean.

Maher, F. A., & Tetreault, M. K. T. (1994). *The feminist classroom: An inside look at how professors and students are transforming higher education for a diverse society.* New York, NY: Basic Books.

Mandernach, B. J. (2009). *Writing a "syllabus version" of your philosophy of teaching.* Retrieved from www.facultyfocus.com

Marquis, E., Healey, M., & Vine, M. (2014). Building capacity for the scholarship of teaching and learning (SoTL) using international collaborative writing groups. *International Journal for the Scholarship of Teaching and Learning, 8*(1), 1–34.

McClellan, D. (1973). Testing for competence rather than for intelligence. *American Psychologist, 28*, 1–14.

McCormack, C., & Kennelly, R. (2011). "We must get together and *really* talk …": Connection, engagement, and safety sustain learning and teaching conversation communities. *Reflective Practice: International and Multidisciplinary Perspectives, 12*, 515–531.

McGranahan, E. (2008). Shaking the "Magic 8 Ball": Reflections of a first-time teacher. *Journal of Teaching in Social Work, 28*, 19–34.

McKeachie, W. J. (2002). *McKeachie's teaching tips: Strategies, research, and theory for college and university teachers* (11th ed.). Boston, MA: Houghton Mifflin.

McKeachie, W. J., & Svinicki, M. (2006). *Teaching tips: Strategies, research, and theory for college and university teachers* (12th ed.). Boston, MA: Houghton Mifflin.

McKinney, K. (2007). *Enhancing learning through the scholarship of teaching and learning: The challenges and joys of juggling.* San Francisco, CA: Anker.

McKinney, K. (Ed.). (2013). *The scholarship of teaching and learning in and across the disciplines.* Bloomington: Indiana University Press.

Medina, M. S., & Draugalis, J. R. (2013). Writing a teaching philosophy: An evidence-based approach. *American Journal of Health-Systems Pharmacy, 70*, 191–193.

Meizlish, D., & Kaplan, M. (2008). Valuing and evaluating teaching in academic hiring: A multidisciplinary, cross-institutional study. *Journal of Higher Education, 79*, 489–512.

Merriam, S. B. (2001). Andragogy self-directed learning: Pillars of adult learning theory. *New Directions for Adult & Continuing Education*, 89, 3–13.

Mezirow, J. (1978). Perspective transformation. *Adult Education Quarterly, 28*, 100–110.

Mezirow, J. (1990). *Fostering critical reflection in adulthood.* New York, NY: Jossey-Bass.

Mezirow, J. (2000). *Learning as transformation: Critical perspectives on a theory in progress.* San Francisco, CA: Jossey Bass.

Mezirow, J. (2003). Transformative learning as discourse. *Journal of Transformative Education, 1*(1), 58–63.

Miller, A. N., Taylor, S. G., & Bedeian, A. G. (2011). Publish or perish: Academic life as management faculty live it. *Career Development International, 16*, 422–445.

Miller, J., Bosk, E., Duron, J., Finno, M., & Abner, K. (2016). The role and impact of peer-learning networks in social work doctoral training. *Journal of Social Work Education, 52*, 360–371. doi:10.1080/10437797.2016.1174632

Miller, J., Eaves, M., & Grise-Owens, E. (2014, March). Using autoethnography to explore and articulate implicit curriculum. Presentation at the annual conference of the Association of Baccalaureate Social Work Program Directors, Louisville, KY.

Miller, J., & Grise-Owens, E. (2008, November). *Teaching – Learning empowerment in a consumerist culture.* Paper presented at the Annual Program Meeting of the Council on Social Work Education, Philadelphia, PA.

Miller, J., Grise-Owens, E., Addison, D, Marshall, M., Trabue, D., & Escobar-Ratliff, L. (2016). Planning an organizational wellness initiative at a multi-state social service organization. *Evaluation and Planning: The International Journal, 56,* 1–10.

Miller, J., Grise-Owens, E., Drury, W., Rickman, C. (In press). Developing a professional writing course using a holistic view of competence. *Journal of Social Work Education.*

Miller, J., Grise-Owens, E., & Escobar-Ratliff, L. (2015.) Preparing students for social work licensure: A curricular case example. *Journal of Teaching in Social Work, 35,* 296–316.

Miller, J., Grise-Owens, E., & Shalash, N. (2018). Investigating the self-care practices of social work faculty: An exploratory study. *Social Work Education.* Advance online publication. doi:10.1080/02615479.2018.1470618

Miller, S. E. (2013). Professional socialization: A bridge between the explicit and implicit curriculum. *Journal of Social Work Education, 49,* 368–386.

Minnich, E. K. (1990). *Transforming knowledge.* Philadelphia, PA: Temple University Press.

Misra, J., Lindquist, J. H., Holmes, E., & Agiomavritis, S. (2001). The ivory ceiling of service work. *Academe, 97*(1), 22–26.

Mitzel, H. (1960). Teacher effectiveness. In C. E. Harris (Ed.), *Encyclopedia of Educational Research* (3rd ed., pp. 1481–1486). New York, NY: Macmillan.

Montell, G. (2011, March 27). *How to write a statement of teaching philosophy.* Retrieved from http://chronicle.com/article/How-to-Write-a-Statement-of/45133/

Moore, K. (2016). Living liminal: Reflexive epistemological positioning at the intersection of marginalized identities. *Qualitative Social Work, 15,* 715–726.

Moore, T. (2012). *Educational theory: An introduction.* New York, NY: Routledge.

Naidoo, R., & Jamieson, I. (2005). Empowering participants or corroding learning? Towards a research agenda on the impact of student consumerism in higher education. *Journal of Education Policy,* 20, 267–281.

National Association of Social Workers. (2017). *Code of ethics.* Retrieved from https://socialwork.utexas.edu/dl/files/academic-programs/other/nasw-code-of-ethics.pdf

O'Brien, J. G., Millis, B. J., & Cohen, M. W. (2008). *The course syllabus: A learning-centered approach* (2nd ed.). San Francisco, CA: Jossey-Bass.

O'Neil, C., Meizlish, D. & Kaplan, M. (2007). *Writing a statement of teaching philosophy for the academic job search* (CRLT Occasional Paper No. 23). Retrieved from http://www.crlt.umich.edu/publinks/CRLT_no23.pdf

Ohito, E. O. (2016). Making the emperor's new clothes visible in anti-racist teacher education: Enacting a pedagogy of discomfort with White preservice teachers. *Equity & Excellence in Education, 49*, 454–467.

Owens, L. W. (2016). Reflections of a pracademic: A journey from social work practitioner to academic. *Reflections: Narratives of Professional Helping, 22*(1), 37–43.

Owens, L. W., Call, C., & Vincent, N. J. (2017). Social work faculty's perceptions of the leadership qualities of their academic leaders. *International Journal of Leadership and Change, 5*(1), 5–29.

Owens, L. W., Miller, J., & Grise-Owens, E. (2014). Activating a teaching philosophy in social work education: Articulation, implementation, and evaluation. *Journal of Teaching in Social Work, 34*, 332–345.

Palmer, C. (2013). *Reflections on teaching: From surviving to thriving*. Retrieved from https://www.facultyfocus.com/articles/faculty-development/reflections-on-teaching-from-surviving-to-thriving/

Palmer, P. J. (1998). *The courage to teach: Exploring the inner landscape of a teacher's life*. San Francisco, CA: Jossey-Bass.

Parini, J. (2005). *The art of teaching*. New York, NY: Oxford University Press.

Paul, R., & Elder, L. (2004). *The miniature guide to critical thinking: Concepts and tools*. Dillon Beach, CA: Foundation for Critical Thinking.

Peters, M. A. (2009). Editorial: A teaching philosophy or philosophy of teaching? *Educational Philosophy and Theory, 41*, 111–113.

Peters, J. K., & Weisberg, M. (2011). *A teacher's reflection book: Exercises, stories, invitations*. Durham, NC: Carolina Academic Press.

Peterson, N. A., Farmer, A. Y., Donnelly, L., & Forenza, B. (2014). Assessing the implicit curriculum in social work education: Heterogeneity of students' experiences and impact of professional empowerment. *Journal of Teaching in Social Work, 34*, 460–479.

Phelps, H. (2014, December 8). Simplify the application process. *Chronicle of Higher Education*. Retrieved from https://www.chronicle.com/article/Simplify-the-Application/150429

Piaget, J. (1970). *The science of education and the psychology of the child*. New York, NY: Grossman.

Pike, B., Bradley, F., & Mansfield, J. (1997). The philosophy of teaching: Developing a statement that thrives in the classroom. *Clearing House, 70*(3), 125–129.

Potts, M. (2005). The consumerist subversion of education. *Academic Questions, 17*, 54–64.

Pratt, D. D. (2005). Personal philosophies of teaching: A false promise? *Academe, 91*(1), 32–35.

Pratt, D., & Collins, J. (2002, November). *International perspectives on teaching: Internationalizing education in the Asia-Pacific region*. Paper presented at the 30th Annual ANZCIES Conference, University of New England, Armadale, New South Wales, Australia.

Pryor, C. R. (2004). *Writing a philosophy of education statement: An educator's workbook* (2nd ed.). Boston, MA: McGraw-Hill.

Pyles, L, & Adam, G. J. (2016). *Holistic engagement: Transformative social work education in the 21st century*. New York, NY: Oxford University Press.

Ratnapradipa, D., & Abrams, T. (2012). Framing the teaching philosophy statement for health educators: What it includes and how it can inform professional development. *Health Educator, 44*(1), 37–42

Reber, J. (2011). The under-examined life: A proposal for critically evaluating teachers' and students' philosophies of teaching. *College Teaching, 59*, 102–110.

Reid, P. T. (2012). Black and female in academia. *The Presidency* (*Suppl. 1*), 6–10.

Reigeluth, C.(1983). Meaningfulness and instruction: Relating what is being learned to what a student knows. *Instructional Science, 12*, 197–218.

Richardson, J., & Swan, K. (2003). Examining social presence in online courses in relation to students' perceived learning and satisfaction. *Journal of Asynchronous Learning Networks, 7*(1), 68–88.

Richlin, L., & Cox, M. (2004). Developing scholarly teaching and the scholarship of teaching and learning through faculty learning communities. *New Directions for Teaching and Learning*, 97, 127–136.

Roche, S. E., Dewees, M., Trailweaver, R., Alexander, S., Cuddy, C., & Handy, M. (1999). *Contesting boundaries in social work education: A liberatory approach to cooperative learning and teaching*. Alexandria, VA: Council on Social Work Education.

Rogers, C.R. (1983). *Freedom to Learn for the 80s*. Columbus, OH: Charles Merrill.

Royse, D. (2001). *Teaching tips for college and university instructors: A practical guide.* Boston: Allyn and Bacon.

Sage, M., & Sele, P. (2015). Reflective journaling as a flipped classroom technique to increase reading and participation with social work students. *Journal of Social Work Education, 51*, 668–681.

Saleebey, D., & Scanlon, E. (2005). Is critical pedagogy for the profession of social work possible? *Journal of Teaching in Social Work, 25*(3/4), 1–18.

Sankey, L. I., & Foster, D. D. (2012). A content analysis of teaching philosophy statements of award winning colleges of agriculture professors. *Journal of Agricultural Education, 53*(4), 124–140.

Saville, B. K., Zinn, T. E., Brown, A. R., & Marchuk, K. A. (2010). Syllabus detail and students' perceptions of teacher effectiveness. *Teaching of Psychology, 37*, 186–189.

Scariono, A., & Liddicoat, A. J. (2009). *Teaching and learning languages: A guide.* Carlton South, Victoria, Australia: Curriculum Corporation.

Schmier, L. (1995). *Random thoughts: The humanity of teaching.* Madison, WI: Magna.

Schön, D. (1983). *The reflective practitioner: How professionals think in action.* London, UK: Temple Smith.

Schönwetter, D. J., Sokal, L., Friesen, M., & Taylor, K. L. (2002). Teaching philosophies reconsidered: A conceptual model for the development and evaluation of teaching philosophy statements. *International Journal for Academic Development, 7*, 83–97.

Schussler, E. E., Rowland, F. E., Distel, C. A., Bauman, J. M., Keppler, M. L., Kawarasaki, Y., … Salem, H. (2011). Promoting the development of graduate students' teaching philosophy statements. *Journal of College Science Teaching, 40*, 32–35.

Seldin, P. (1991). *The teaching portfolio: A practical guide to improved performance and promotion/tenure decisions.* Boston, MA: Anker.

Seldin, P., & Associates (1993) *Successful use of teaching portfolios.* Bolton, MA: Anker.

Shulman, L.S. (2000). From Minsk to Pinsk: Why a scholarship of teaching and learning? *Journal of Scholarship of Teaching and Learning, 1*(1), 48–52.

Shulman, L. S. (2004). *Teaching as community property: Essays on higher education.* San Francisco, CA: Jossey-Bass.

Skinner, B. F. (1953). *Science and human behavior.* New York, NY: Macmillan.

Skinner, B. F. (1954). *Cooperative learning.* (2nd ed). Boston, MA: Allyn & Bacon.

Skinner, B. F. (1974.) *About behaviorism.* San Francisco, CA: Knopf.

Skovholt, T. M., & Trotter-Mathison, M. (2011). *The resilient practitioner—Burnout prevention and self-care strategies for counselors, therapists, teachers, and health professionals.* New York, NY: Routledge.

Slišković, A., & Seršić, D. M. (2011). Work stress among university teachers: Gender and Position differences. *Archives of Industrial Hygiene and Toxicology, 62*, 299–307.

Smith, B. P. (2009). Student ratings of teaching effectiveness for faculty groups based on race and gender. *Education, 129*, 615–624.

Stamm, J. (1997). Philosophy of education workbook: Writing a statement of beliefs and practices. New York, NY: McGall-Hill.

Steele, C. M., Spencer, C. J., & Aronson, J. (2002). Contending with group image: The psychology of stereotype and social identity threat. *Advances in Experimental Social Psychology, 34*, 379–440.

Stenhouse, L. (1975). *An introduction to curriculum research and development.* London, UK: Heinemann.

Stevens, D. D., & Levi, A. (2005). *Introduction to rubrics: An assessment tool to save grading time, convey effective feedback, and promote student learning.* Sterling, VA: Stylus.

Stonebraker, R. J. & Stone, G. S. (2015). Too old to teach? The effect of age on college and university professors. *Research in Higher Education, 56*, 793–812.

Storage, D., Home, Z, Cimpian, A., & Leslie, S. (2015). The frequency of "brilliant" and "genius" in teaching evaluations predicts the representation of women and African Americans across field. *PLoS ONE, 11*(3), 1–17.

Sustain. (n.d.). In *Merriam-Webster's online dictionary* (11th ed.). Retrieved from https://www.merriam-webster.com/dictionary/sustain

Svinicki, M. D., & McKeachie, W. J. (2014). *Mckeachie's teaching tips: Strategies, research, and theory for college and university teachers* (14th ed.). Belmont, CA: Wadsworth, Cengage Learning.

Teater, B. A., (2011). Maximizing student learning: A case example of applying teaching learning theory in social work education. *Social Work Education, 30*, 571–585.

Theobald, J., Gardner, F., & Long, N. (2017). Teaching critical reflection in social work field education. *Journal of Social Work Education, 53*, 300–311.

Turner, C. S. V., Gonzalez, J. C., & Wood, J. L. (2008). Faculty of color in academe: What 20 years of literature tells us. *Journal of Diversity in Higher Education, 1*, 139–168.

Van Soest, D., & Garcia, B. (2003). *Diversity education for social justice: Mastering teaching skills*. Alexandra, VA: CSWE Press.

Vella, J. (2002). *Learning to listen, learning to teach: The power of dialogue in educating adults.* San Francisco, CA: Jossey-Bass.

Vescio, V., Ross, D., Adams, A. (2008). A review of research on the impact of professional learning communities on teaching practices and student learning. *Teaching and Teacher Education, 24*(1), 80–91.

Vygotsky, L. S. (1978). *Mind and society: The development of higher mental processes*. Cambridge, MA: Harvard University Press.

Wagner, N., Rieger, M., & Voorvelt, K. (2016). Gender, ethnicity and teaching evaluations: Evidence from mixed teaching teams. *Economics of Education Review, 54*, 79–94.

Walvoord, B. E. & Anderson, V. J. (2010). *Effective grading: A tool for learning and assessment.* San Francisco, CA: Jossey-Bass.

Wang, D. (2012). The use of self and reflective practice in relational teaching and adult learning: A social work perspective. *Reflective Practice, 13*(1), 55–63.

Watson, J. B. (1928). *The ways of behaviorism*. Oxford, UK: Harper.

Watson, J. B. (1930). *Behaviorism* (Rev. ed.). New York, NY: Norton.

Webb, L. M., Allen, M. W., & Walker, K. L. (2002) Feminist pedagogy: Identifying basic principles. *Academic Exchange Quarterly, 6*, 67–72

Wehbi, S. (2009). Reclaiming our agency in academia: Engaging in the scholarship of teaching in social work. *Social Work Education, 28*, 502–511.

Weimer, M. (2002). *Learner-centered teaching: Five key changes to practice.* San Francisco, CA: Jossey-Bass.

Weimer, M. (2006). *Enhancing scholarly work on teaching and learning: Professional literature that makes a difference.* San Francisco, CA: Jossey-Bass.

Weimer, M. (2010). *Inspired college teaching: A career-long resource for professional growth.* San Francisco, CA: Jossey-Bass.

Weimer, M. (2013). *Teaching strategies for the college classroom: A collection of faculty articles.* Madison, WI: Magna.

Weinstein, C. E., Meyer, D. K., Husman, J., Van Mater Stone, G., & McKeachie, W. J. (2006). Teaching students how to become more strategic and self-regulated learners. In W. J. McKeachie, & M. Svinicki (Eds.), *McKeachie's teaching tips: Strategies, research, and theory for college and university teachers* (pp. 300–317). Boston, MA: Houghton Mifflin.

Weisenberg, F., & Stacey, E. (2005). Reflections on teaching and learning online: Quality program design, delivery, and support issues from a cross-global perspective. *Distance Education, 26*, 385–404.

Werder, C., & Otis, M. M. (Eds.). (2010). *Engaging student voices in the study of teaching and learning.* Sterling, VA: Stylus.

Western Kentucky University (n.d.). *About WKU.* Retrieved from https://www.wku.edu/international/about_wku.php.

Wilson, P. P., Valentine, D., & Pereira, A. (2002). Perceptions of new social work faculty about mentoring experiences. *Journal of Social Work Education, 38*, 317–332.

Winans-Solis, J. (2014). Reclaiming power and identity: Marginalized students' experiences of service-learning. *Equity & Excellence in Education, 47*, 604–621.

Witkin, S. L. (2014). Change and deeper change: Transforming social work education. *Journal of Social Work Education, 50*, 587–598.

Witkin, S. L., & Saleebey, D. (Eds.). (2007). *Social work dialogues: Transforming the canon of inquiry, practice, and education.* Alexandria, VA: Council on Social Work Education.

Wood, T. & McCarthy, C. (2002). Understanding and preventing teacher burnout. Retrieved from https://www.ericdigests.org/2004-1/burnout.htm

Yale Center for Clinical Investigation (n.d.). *Beyond scientific publication: Strategies for disseminating research findings.* Retrieved from https://depts.washington.edu/ccph/pdf_files/CARE_Dissemination_Strategies_FINAL_eversion.pdf.

Zapf, K. M., Jerome, L., & Williams, M. (2011). Team teaching in social work: Sharing power with bachelor of social work students. *Journal of Teaching in Social Work Education, 31*(1), 38–52.

Resources on Teaching Philosophy Statements

Resources are abundantly available on crafting a teaching philosophy statement. Many universities and colleges have centers on teaching and learning, which often have resources for students and faculty on developing a teaching philosophy statement. We have selected several websites that have information on developing a statement and samples of teaching philosophy statements.

Chronicle of Higher Education
How to Writing a Statement of Teaching Philosophy, Gabriela Montell
http://www.chronicle.com/article/How-to-Write-a-Statement-of/45133/

Chronicle of Higher Education
Writing Samples and Teaching Statements, Julie Miller Vick and Jennifer S. Furlong
http://www.chronicle.com/article/Writing-SamplesTeaching/125726/

Cornell University Graduate School: Pathways to Success
Teaching Philosophy Statement
http://gradschool.cornell.edu/pathways-success/prepare-your-career/career-guide/teaching-philosophy-statement

Duquesne University: Center for Teaching Excellence
Statement of Teaching Philosophy
http://www.duq.edu/about/centers-and-institutes/center-for-teaching-excellence/academic-careers/landing-an-academic-job/statement-of-teaching-philosophy

Ohio State University: University Center for the Advancement of Teaching
Whiting a Philosophy of Teaching Statement
https://ucat.osu.edu/professional-development/teaching-portfolio/philosophy/

University of Calgary: Taylor Institute for Teaching and Learning
Sample Teaching Philosophy Statements
http://ucalgary.ca/taylorinstitute/resources/teaching-philosophies-dossiers/sample-teaching-philosophy-statements

University of Central Florida: Karen L. Smith Faculty Center for Teaching and Learning
Sample Teaching Philosophies
http://www.fctl.ucf.edu/facultysuccess/professionalportfolios/philosophies.php

University of Calgary: Taylor Institute for Teaching and Learning
Sample Teaching Philosophy Statements
http://ucalgary.ca/taylorinstitute/resources/teaching-philosophies-dossiers/sample-teaching-philosophy-statements

University of Connecticut: Center for Excellence in Teaching and Learning
Teaching Philosophy
https://cetl.uconn.edu/teaching-philosophy/

University of Michigan: Center for Research on Learning and Teaching
Teaching Philosophies from U-M
http://www.crlt.umich.edu/tstrategies/tstpum

University of Minnesota: Center for Educational Innovation
Writing a Teaching Philosophy
https://cei.umn.edu/support-services/tutorials/writing-teaching-philosophy

Vanderbilt University: Center for Teaching
Teaching Statements
https://cft.vanderbilt.edu/guides-sub-pages/teaching-statements/

Appendix B

Sample Teaching Philosophies

Teaching With *E*s Leads to Educational Excellence
Erlene Grise-Owens

My teaching–learning philosophy is encapsulated in five *E*s. My philosophy is integrally connected with the university mission (see Figure A1). The following is a succinct description of the activation of my philosophy and its linkage with the university mission. This activation is discussed further in my academic review documents and SoTL products (see CV).

Empowering: All educational processes should be empowering to all parties. This belief mirrors the social work profession's core principles and the university mission's emphasis on promotion of peace and justice. Empowerment means equitably shared responsibilities and rights. One of myriad ways I enact this *E* is through my often stated mantra, High standards, high supports. One concrete way is through my critical, constructive, clear, and timely feedback and explicit use of student feedback. Consistently I see students hold themselves to high standards and achieve in ways beyond their initial expectations.

Engaging: Effective and meaningful teaching–learning actively engages a diverse community of learners. This engagement means having the skills and strategies to ensure all voices are heard, not just the dominant and privileged. I model this *E* through taking a guide on the side facilitative approach, contrasted with a sage on the stage approach. I practice this *E* by being explicit about power dynamics in the classroom, such as facilitating the development of group guidelines. In feedback, students comment about how we engage constructively in conflictual and difficult conversations and how this models professional conduct.

Energizing: Teaching–learning is energizing through being grounded in spiritual values. I define spirituality as the process of meaning making and enact this *E* using

Figure A1. Teaching with Es Leads to Educational Excellence
Erlene Grise-Owens

University Mission Statement

The university is a diverse community of learners dedicated to meeting the needs of the times in the tradition of the Sisters of Charity of Nazareth through quality undergraduate and graduate liberal and professional studies, grounded in spiritual values, with emphasis on service and the promotion of peace and justice.

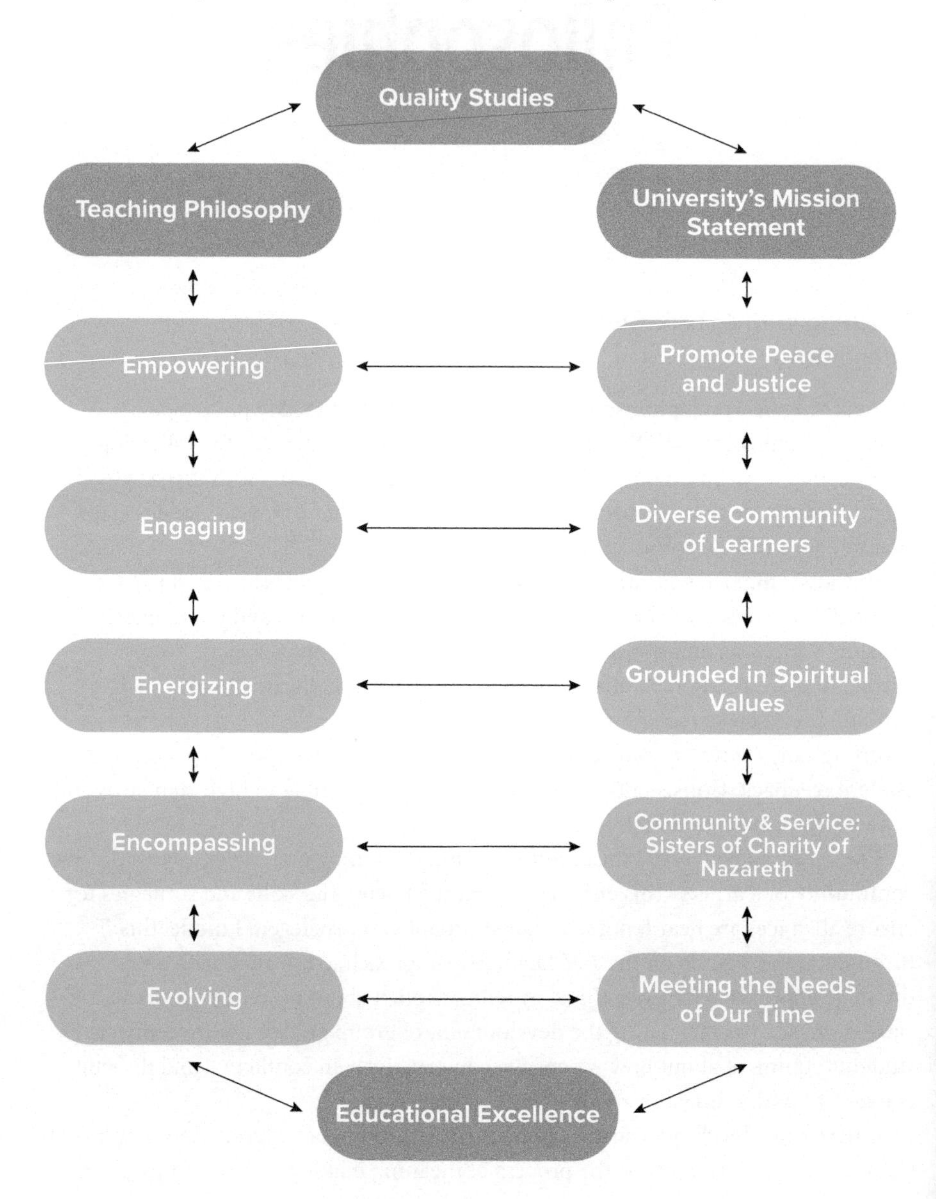

transformative and active learning principles and a liberatory approach. From the syllabus design, to every interaction and assignment, I promote meaningful connections between the students and the content of the course and among the people in the course. For example, many of my assignments use self-reflection and peer reviews. Students comment about their growing self-confidence and connection to the values of the profession.

Encompassing: In the tradition of the Sisters of Charity of Nazareth, I believe the ultimate aim of education is to serve a higher purpose and build community. Thus, I connect the course and our teaching–learning community with the broader world. To build community throughout my courses, students share their theme songs. In the first class, I frame our experience as encompassing with my theme song, "What a Wonderful World." I articulate that as a microcosm of the world. Also, I see my role as encompassing, beyond the classroom. I enact this *E* through mentoring students in their professional growth. For instance, I initiated a scholarship interest group of students and alumni, which contributed to various scholarship products. This collegial productivity is a measure of encompassing.

Evolving: This final *E* represents meeting the needs of the times in the global sense and the immediate sense. I continuously improve my teaching. For instance, I explicitly use formative and summative feedback in my courses and convey that usage to students. More broadly, a primary way I meet this facet is through my active professional involvement, which keeps me apprised of the changes in our complex profession and the ever-evolving landscape of education. ■

Statement of Teaching–Learning Philosophy

Justin "Jay" Miller

I practice a liberatory approach to teaching and learning. Liberatory is a process defined as, "tending to set free . . . To be liberatory is to construct, in concert with others, the conditions and to engage in the critical inquiry and connective dialogue that makes liberation more likely" (Roche et al., 1999, p. xiii). This definition serves as the foundation for my teaching–learning philosophy. I have adopted a teaching philosophy I call liberatory teaching-learning (Miller & Grise-Owens, 2008, 2009; Owens, Miller, & Grise-Owens, 2014). This approach was initially inspired by Roche et al. (1999), which was coauthored by faculty and students. My approach is further rooted in transformative active learning and experiential and criticalist learning theories and has been influenced by the seminal works of Dewey (1938), Freire (1998, 2007), Kolb (1984), and Mezirow (1990). My philosophy emphasizes coconstructed knowledge (e.g., teacher-learner partnerships) and views the classroom as a microcosm of the broader world (Birkenmaier et al., 2011; Fox, 2013; Goldstein, 2001; Grise-Owens, Miller, & Owens, 2016; hooks, 2003; Saleebey & Scanlon, 2005).

Principles of Liberatory Teaching and Learning

Liberatory teaching and learning, in practice, encapsulates a holistic experience of the education process. There are three distinct principles of this approach that revolve around a central premise: The classroom is a community of participants. Barker (2003) defined a community as a group of individuals who share and invest in a distinct value set. Bain (2004) asserted that optimal teaching operates on a similar premise that everyone works in unison toward a common goal. Developing a nourishing sense of community is perhaps the most important aspect of teaching (McKeachie & Svinicki, 2006). Classroom environments offer the best potential for learning when they operate as a healthy, united community (Svinicki & McKeachie, 2014). The following is a synopsis of liberatory teaching and learning principles that serve to create this community.

Participants in this approach are interdependent colearners. hooks (2003) contended that a true sense of community transcends the traditional hierarchical culture of dominance. Thus, participants of a learning community recognize that everyone has varying, but significant, expertise and life experiences. Learning communities draw on these unique gifts to build a sense of community. In turn, these experiences serve as a catalyst for deeper and more sustained learning opportunities.

Power dynamics are made explicit. In the liberatory teaching and learning approach, it is apposite that power dynamics are made explicit. This concept refers to the dynamic between the teacher and the student. Several practical strategies make these power dynamics explicit. Anecdotally, I have found that language (i.e., semantics) is the most important. For example, I try to be careful about the terms I use in class, for example, students *earn* grades as opposed to *getting* grades, and they are *contributing to* or *investigating knowledge* and not being *given* knowledge. By naming the power dynamic, expectations and mutual accountability measures are made clear, thus, ensuring effective communication between the participants in the learning community.

Dialogical praxis is a necessary component of all healthy communities, learning and otherwise. Dialogical praxis refers to a reciprocal and mutually informing dialogue among the participants of the learning community. For the members of the community to have their learning needs met—as well as have the opportunity to contribute—clear lines of communication must be established. Thus, my approach to classroom instruction centers on more dialogue than lecture. Similarly my grading practices take into account multiple perspectives; for example, I routinely use peer reviews, self-assessments, participatory feedback, and so forth.

Products of Liberatory Teaching and Learning

An activated, effective teaching philosophy must articulate clear goals, or desired products and outcomes. My approach to teaching and learning yields several observable products. The following paragraphs outline three of the outcomes associated with my approach.

Co-Constructed Knowledge

Askeland and Payne (2006) asserted that "social work education needs to be reframed as a process of emergence in which educators and students work jointly to create knowledge and identity in their professional arena" (p. 167). I approach the conceptualization and development of the social work knowledge base as a shared endeavor in which all members of the learning community, individually and collaboratively, share responsibility and accountability. This mutually constructed framework fosters a motivation to learn, seek, and cultivate knowledge and serves to ensure sound practice decision making, which promotes competent practice.

Revisioned (Redefined) Classroom

My liberatory teaching and learning approach offers a distinctive view on the classroom that is counter to traditional methods of teaching and learning (i.e., Freire's, 2007, banking model of education). Traditional methods of classroom instruction often views the student as an empty being that needs to be filled and that teaching–learning processes only flow one way (from the teacher to the student). My approach to teaching and learning recognizes that everyone has something to contribute to the community and that students' knowledge and experiences have merit and value in the education process.

Human Rights and Social Change

My teaching approach mirrors pertinent dynamics associated with social work practice. For example, my liberatory teaching and learning approach values the dignity and worth of each member of the learning community and recognizes the importance of relationships among members of the community. Additionally, this method also brings about mutual accountability, which fosters a more strategic and engaged learning experience (Witkin & Saleebey, 2007). In turn, students are encouraged and are more able to engage in and promote social change.

Possibilities of Liberatory Teaching and Learning

My teaching–learning approach offers several unique educational possibilities. First, by optimizing learning through diversification, methods of learning become foundational rather than concrete. This approach allows a flexible education system that can adapt to constantly evolving methods and practices. Second, with the liberatory approach, the dialogue power related to the investigation of knowledge expands, which means that the classroom becomes learning centered, not learner centered, and students become more confident and competent. Third, this approach promotes the possibility of increased camaraderie and collaboration in the learning community, which strengthens relationships and extends the traditional classroom boundaries. In turn, increased synergy in the learning environment results, which organically feeds the ongoing teaching and learning.

Conclusion

Developing, articulating, and implementing a teaching philosophy requires intentionality. Inherently, being intentional about using this philosophy, and sharing it in the learning community requires for me to be vulnerable, flexible, and open to critical feedback pertaining to the philosophy. Although I am committed to my teaching philosophy, my philosophy is living and fluid. ■

Teaching–Learning Philosophy

Larry W. Owens

My teaching–learning philosophy is grounded in 25 years of social work practice experience, educational leadership principles, and personal commitment to global citizenship. I bring extensive practice skills, including training and staff development. A particular strength I have is the ability to link the perspective of an administrator and practitioner who hired and supervised various levels of staff with the role of teacher who prepares students to enter the workforce and positively affect our society. I agree with bell hook's (2003) assertion that effective teaching engages the "world as classroom" (p. xx).

My teaching philosophy emphasizes the following complementary and interrelated dimensions.

Integrative Framework

My teaching integrates theory, practice skills, critical thinking, and communication. Two of the most important skills needed in the professional setting are the abilities to think critically and communicate clearly. Also, I value a liberal arts education and the integration of multiple disciplines and perspectives in a holistic higher educational experience.

Relevant Application

A primary goal of my teaching is to make course content relevant and applicable to the practice setting and cultural context. Theory without practice applicability is limiting. Practice without theoretical grounding is superficial and shallow. Learning is stimulated best by connections between content and lived contexts.

Supportive Mentoring

As an administrator and supervisor, I mentored numerous new professionals in the human services field. As a field placement and practicum supervisor, a primary role was encouraging students as they develop confidence and competence in their professional identities. I view supportive mentoring as a primary function of the faculty role.

Communication Emphasis

An effective practitioner must be able to communicate verbally and in writing. The ability to communicate effectively is closely linked with the ability to think critically. Likewise, effective communication involves modifying the communication for the intended audience. Culturally competent communication is particularly relevant for multicultural settings and an increasingly global context. Similarly, communication is integral to effective collaboration, which is a core competency in today's workplace.

Interactive Approach

My teaching involves engaged interaction between learners and instructor. A primary means of learning involves interacting with new information and digesting and applying it to current situations. Interactive learning fosters teamwork among learners, which is a primary skill needed in the practice setting. ■

Links Between Professional Competencies and Teaching Philosophy

Table 1 illustrates how to link components of a teaching philosophy with professional educational competencies of the CSWE (2015) and the Interprofessional Education Collaborative Competencies (2016). The CSWE designates nine professional competencies, and IPEC specifies four core competencies. This table uses Larry's teaching philosophy to illustrate the linkage. The links will vary depending on the particular components of your teaching philosophy and your discipline's professional competencies or standards.

Table 1. Linking Teaching Philosophy With Educational Competencies

Larry's Teaching Philosophy	Council on Social Work Education (2015)	Interprofessional Education Collaborative (2016)
Integrative framework My teaching integrates theory, practice skills, critical thinking, and communication. Two of the most important skills needed in the professional setting are the abilities to think critically and communicate clearly. Also, I value liberal arts education and the integration of multiple disciplines and perspectives in a holistic higher educational experience.	**Competency 1:** Demonstrate ethical and professional behavior **Competency 4:** Engage in practice-informed research and research-informed practice	**Values, ethics:** Work with individuals of other professions to maintain a climate of mutual respect and shared values **Roles, responsibilities:** Use the knowledge of one's own role and those of other professions to appropriately assess and address the health care needs of patients and to promote and advance the health of populations **Interprofessional communication:** Communicate with patients, families, communities, and professionals in health and other fields in a responsive and responsible manner that supports a team approach to the promotion and maintenance of health and the prevention and treatment of disease

Larry's Teaching Philosophy	Council on Social Work Education (2015)	Interprofessional Education Collaborative (2016)
Relevant application: A primary goal of my teaching is to make course content relevant and applicable to the practice setting and cultural context. Theory without practice applicability is limiting. Practice without theoretical grounding is superficial and shallow. Learning is stimulated best by connections between content and lived contexts.	**Competency 2:** Engage diversity and difference in practice **Competency 4:** Engage in Practice-informed research and research-informed Practice **Competency 5:** Engage in policy practice **Competency 7:** Assess individuals, families, groups, organizations, and communities **Competency 8:** Intervene with individuals, families, groups, organizations, and communities **Competency 9:** Evaluate practice with individuals, families, groups, organizations, and communities	**Values, ethics:** Work with individuals of other professions to maintain a climate of mutual respect and shared values **Roles, responsibilities:** Use the knowledge of one's own role and those of other professions to appropriately assess and address the health care needs of patients and to promote and advance the health of populations **Teams and teamwork:** Apply relationship-building values and the principles of team dynamics to perform effectively in different team roles to plan, deliver, and evaluate patient- or population-centered care and population health programs and policies that are safe, timely, efficient, effective, and equitable.

Larry's Teaching Philosophy	Council on Social Work Education (2015)	Interprofessional Education Collaborative (2016)
Supportive mentoring: As a past social work administrator and supervisor, I mentored numerous new professionals in the human services field. As a field placement and practicum supervisor, I encouraged students to develop confidence and competence in their professional identities. I view my current role as social work educator as a continuation of the mentoring relationship.	**Competency 1:** Demonstrate ethical and professional behavior **Competency 6:** Engage with individuals, families, groups, organizations, and communities **Competency 8:** Intervene with individuals, families, groups, organizations, and communities	**Roles, responsibilities:** Use the knowledge of one's own role and those of other professions to appropriately assess and address the health care needs of patients and to promote and advance the health of populations

Larry's Teaching Philosophy	Council on Social Work Education (2015)	Interprofessional Education Collaborative (2016)
Communication emphasis: An effective practitioner must be able to communicate verbally and in writing. The ability to communicate effectively is closely linked with the ability to think critically. Likewise, effective communication involves modifying the communication for the intended audience. Culturally competent communication is particularly relevant for multicultural settings and an increasingly global context. Similarly, communication is integral to effective collaboration, which is a core competency in today's workplace.	**Competency 2:** Engage diversity and difference in practice **Competency 3:** Advance human rights and social, economic, and environmental justice **Competency 8:** Intervene with individuals, families, groups, organizations, and communities	**Roles, responsibilities:** Use the knowledge of one's own role and those of other professions to appropriately assess and address the health care needs of patients and to promote and advance the health of populations Interprofessional communication: Communicate with patients, families, communities, and professionals in health and other fields in a responsive and responsible manner that supports a team approach to the promotion and maintenance of health and the prevention and treatment of disease

Larry's Teaching Philosophy	Council on Social Work Education (2015)	Interprofessional Education Collaborative (2016)
Interactive approach: My teaching involves engaged interaction between learners and instructor. A primary means of learning involves interacting with the new information and digesting and applying it to current situations. Interactive learning fosters teamwork among learners, which is a primary skill needed in the social work practice setting.	**Competency 6:** Engage with individuals, families, groups, organizations, and communities **Competency 6:** Engage with individuals, families, groups, organizations, and communities **Competency 8:** Intervene with individuals, families, groups, organizations, and communities	**Roles, responsibilities:** Use the knowledge of one's own role and those of other professions to appropriately assess and address the health care needs of patients and to promote and advance the health of populations **Teams and teamwork:** Apply relationship-building values and the principles of team dynamics to perform effectively in different team roles to plan, deliver, and evaluate patient- and population-centered care and population health programs and policies that are safe, timely, efficient, effective, and equitable

Index

B

C

About the Authors

Erlene Grise-Owens, EdD, LCSW, MSW, MRE, is partner in The Wellness Group, ETC. This LLC provides evaluation, training, and consultation on practitioner self-care and organizational wellness. Erlene taught for more than two decades in social work education, achieving the rank of full professor. During that time, she served as director of field education and graduate program director. Erlene also worked in administrative and direct practice roles in community and agency practice arenas, including child welfare, behavioral health, and religious-affiliated contexts. Erlene has substantive scholarship, particularly in scholarship of teaching–learning and self-care/wellness in the helping professions. At this point in her career, Erlene is focused on promoting well-being in the helping professions, including higher education.

J. Jay Miller, PhD, MSW, CSW, is the associate dean for research, associate professor, and founding director of the Self-Care Lab in the College of Social Work at the University of Kentucky. Jay's research and academic interests include child welfare, self-care as a professional practice skill, and scholarship of teaching–learning. Jay currently serves as the chair of Kentucky's Juvenile Justice Advisory Board, Board of Social Work, and Children's Justice Act Taskforce. Jay is a past recipient of the Cabinet for Health and Family Services' Paul Grannis Award and is a 2014 inductee into the College of Health and Human Services Hall of Fame at Western Kentucky University. Last but not least, Jay is a proud foster and kin care alum!

Larry W. Owens, EdD, MSW, CSW, is associate professor of social work at Western Kentucky University (WKU). He is the lead faculty member at the WKU Elizabethtown Regional Campus. Beginning as a child care worker, Larry has more than 25 years of direct care, clinical, and administrative experience. His experience included working in outpatient mental health services, foster care, group homes, residential treatment, emergency shelters, adoption, and independent living services. Larry's research interests include scholarship of teaching–learning, education at branch campuses, and leadership in the helping professions. He is particularly committed to global educational experiences and was recently selected as faculty for Semester at Sea.